praise for *a m*

"Frank, funny, and full of a
adeptly flags the challenges
takes aim at everything froi
redefining the concept of the dual career couple. Willing to
share her most intimate thoughts, frustrations, and foibles,
she is the guru of the relocation industry. I will recommend it
to my friends and clients. Bravo!"

~ PAM PERRAUD, PRESIDENT, GLOBAL TRANSITIONS, AND
FOUNDER OF WOMEN ON THE MOVE CONFERENCE

"Robin Pascoe has written a gutsy, forthright look at relocation.
There is no politically correct veneer here. Pascoe says outright
what others discuss in hushed tones. It's a must-read for any
couple thinking about making the leap to expatriate life."

~ TRACEY McTAGUE, SCHLUMBERGER SPOUSECONNECT,
HOUSTON, TEXAS

"Robin may have written *A Moveable Marriage* for spouses
struggling to find their old—or new—identity before, during,
and after a relocation, but it's good, solid, and helpful reading
for anyone whose marriage has lost some luster and needs to
shine again."

~ FRANCESCA KELLY, U.S. STATE DEPARTMENT SPOUSE AND
EDITOR-IN-CHIEF, TALES FROM A SMALL PLANET

"Big business beware: Pascoe takes no prisoners, and her
scathing denunciation of corporate failure to support and
nurture families of their relocating employees may forever
remove the 'human' from human resources."

~ MARY VAN DER BOON, MANAGING DIRECTOR,
GLOBAL TMC INTERNATIONAL

"Robin Pascoe has done it again! *A Moveable Marriage* is a
wonderful description of the bittersweet experiences of the
mobile family. Robin has provided us with a track to follow
and some excellent advice on how to keep hearth and home
together when transporting it across the world."

~ CARRIE SHEARER, PRESIDENT, SHEARER & ASSOCIATES
INTERNATIONAL HR CONSULTING

a moveable
marriage

ALSO BY ROBIN PASCOE

Culture Shock! Successful Living Abroad:
A Wife's Guide

Culture Shock! Successful Living Abroad:
A Parent's Guide

Homeward Bound:
A Spouse's Guide to Repatriation

Relocate Your
Relationship without
Breaking It

a moveable
marriage

ROBIN PASCOE

Expatriate Press

Vancouver

Expatriate Press Limited

1430 Terrace Avenue
North Vancouver, BC
Canada V7R 1B4
(604) 990-4532 (tel)
(604) 990-4598 (fax)
www.expatexpert.com
rpascoe@expatexpert.com

ISBN: 0-9686760-2-2

Edited by Barbara Pulling
Copyedited by Naomi Pauls
Cover and text design by Gabi Proctor/DesignGeist
Cover images by Getty Images
Author photo by Liza Linklater
Printed and bound in Canada

Always and forever, for Rodney

contents

foreword

Books about marriage abound. Any bookstore offers numerous titles on how to assess your marriage, how to know if it isn't working, and how to fix every type of problem in ten easy steps. Often, however, all this information only leaves the reader feeling inadequate and frustrated. Thankfully, this is not one of those books.

Instead, in *A Moveable Marriage,* Robin Pascoe opens her heart and her literary hearth, allowing us to hear the reality and humanity of a good marriage. These pages are not pages filled with myths of perfect communication and ecstasy. Although those moments happen, the highlights of the book are her stories of the tensions and compromises, the array of emotions and doubts and bouts of insecurity that accompany every life and long-term relationship.

By telling us her story, Robin invites us to voice our own stories, so that they don't remain hidden, festering and eventually wounding us. Nothing is taboo here. There are no false smiles masking hidden agendas. We can identify with Robin's ongoing journey through a shared life every step of the way.

Perhaps more importantly, when Robin offers suggestions to help you get through rough times, she is speaking from her experience, not from theory. Theory can be useful. Certainly, as a trained therapist, I have been steeped in theories, and I continue to read and think about them. But it's reality that touches a heart, often opening the way for us to consider and remedy our own situations.

All too often, couples wait until one of them is at the breaking or leaving point before they really look at their situation. Nothing is more heartbreaking in my experience both as a therapist and, before that, as a lawyer than the moment when the couple who has left it too late finally sees the waste of their energy, love, life, and happiness. Even if it's possible to repair the relationship, wounding words and actions have festered, making it more difficult for them to heal over.

Couples leave it too late for many reasons. This book seeks to address many of the obstacles two people face in confronting problems that can eventually ruin a good thing. We all choose how to deal with our lives. We choose, in a myriad of small and larger ways, whether or not to stay married every day. We choose what we say, how we say it, how we show our feelings and our concern for the other person. This is not a book that tells you what to do. But I often find in my practice that people don't know how to be other than how they are. There are no real working models. That's one reason this book is so valuable—you can use it as a working model.

Be careful not to simply copy what you read, though. As Robin points out over and over again, each marriage is unique. In every marriage, two distinct individuals come together to form a relationship that no one else has ever had before. There may be common patterns in relationships and many similarities, but the nuances and intricate needs of each will differ. Still, there is much we can learn from being the proverbial fly on the wall, observing someone else's life and challenges.

Many readers may be amazed at the range of emotions Robin describes as she recounts rages and tantrums, frustrations and insecurities. This can bewilder couples who "never fight." But what is unspoken, and may be felt to be unarguable, can lead to disconnect, fear, disharmony, and retreat from unity in a relationship.

This book, though originally written expressly for the expatriate, actually tells the story of *every* marriage. A relocation serves to highlight what every couple faces in working things out, and it acts as a metaphor for the changes that life constantly throws at us in one form or another, changes that require adjustment and sometimes recovery.

No marriage, or life, is static, however much we might wish that things would stay the same. People change. Some marriages can't handle transformations and growth. "She's not the girl I married," a husband might be heard to say of the sixty-five-year-old woman next to him. What is he thinking? Of course she isn't! What that phrase means to him, however, and how it plays out in the couple's life and expectations of one another can provide clues to the problems that have occurred in the relationship over time.

We all know the statistics on marriage and divorce. What we may not realize is that, in many cases, the failure of a marriage stems not from an impossible situation but from the couple's inability to work things through. The glue that holds a marriage together may not be visible. Often, it isn't the big things that make a relationship work. Over and over again, it can be the invisible dynamics that are the most potent.

Silence is one of the most important and sexy things a couple can offer each other, when it means listening carefully, trying to understand the other person's real feelings and the true meaning of what is being said. Too often, words are used to dominate, to give one person the immediate satisfaction of hurting the other, or to employ the myriad of ploys and recriminations that sidestep caring and sharing.

Watch for the part of the story where Robin's husband helps her with her website, supporting her in a situation where she feels less than able. It seems so simple, but this kind of support is not as common as it should be. It's also evidence of the commitment Robin and her partner have to each other's continued growth as individuals.

This is not to say that silence is completely golden, of course. It's only one of the binding metals that strengthen the relationship. Silver medals (always remember that any humor is better than none!) go out to the couple who are careful to voice and show their caring and concern for one another. From independent bank accounts to a small touch and well-meant "Welcome home," there are many ways to show the other person how much he or she means to you.

Many of the stories in this book contain another essential piece of wisdom, too. In an ideal marriage, we do not merge but maintain our separateness and differing ideas. Our individual identities insulate us when disagreements and conflicts occur. They give us fortitude to face the differences that are a natural part of living together.

Perhaps the most important idea to keep in mind when things feel rough or lonely after a relocation is that, when handled properly, your challenges help your marriage to become stronger. There is a little town in Germany, someone once told me, where people celebrate the first fight between friends, after they have made up. The celebration is for the strength and safety that comes with knowing you can fight and continue to love. Robin's own story is ample evidence of this.

As I read this book, I felt I was in the company of an intelligent, funny, open, and dear friend. I hope you'll have the same enjoyable experience. Sit down with a cup of coffee and share the words of someone who cares about how you are doing.

Phyllis Adler, M.A., J.D., is an American therapist based in London, England. She has a special interest in marriage, business relationships, and communication.

acknowledgments

A Moveable Marriage couldn't have been written without the support of hundreds of women around the world who trusted me with their stories about the emotional impact of their relocation experiences on their relationships. I'm grateful for their honest and insightful contributions to this topic.

I would also like to thank my Vancouver-based editor, Barbara Pulling, who kept me going when I wanted to give up writing this complex and highly charged story of marriages forced to move. Barbara reminded me often that there'll be both good and bad writing days, and that the key to my success was to get over the bad ones quickly and look forward to the good. That's become a valuable lesson for both my writing and my life in general, and certainly an applicable one to women rebuilding lives in strange new cities and countries.

Finally, as always, I want to acknowledge the tremendous support, encouragement, and unconditional love I receive from my family and especially my husband, Rodney. How could I ever have written about a moveable marriage if not for my own happy one to guide me?

introduction

It was literally high noon. I was drenched in sweat, standing on the third-floor landing of an unfamiliar apartment building in a new city, tightly gripping what felt like the hundredth moving box I had emptied out on a scorching summer morning.

Contemplating a cool shower, I was interrupted by my partner. Suited up in his brand-new diplomat's pin-stripe uniform, he'd rushed home from the office to share *great news!* Although we were barely recovering from our first domestic relocation, from Winnipeg to Ottawa, he'd just that morning received word of an international posting in twelve weeks' time, to New York City. *(Isn't that fantastic, honey?)* All we had to do was finish unpacking, find someone to sublet our apartment during his temporary assignment at the United Nations, and get married somewhere along the way.

I did the first thing that popped into my mind: I cried.

IF YOU HAVE PICKED up this book, it probably means that your marriage—and your life—have been transplanted to another place for your husband's job. You

1

may have had a little cry yourself as you packed up your belongings and left your friends behind. Or maybe your move is still imminent. Either way, I'm here to reassure you that you are not going crazy if you feel upset or scared or nervous (possibly all three) and are maybe even beginning to wonder what you saw in the guy in the first place.

Most women don't think much beforehand about the impact a relocation is going to have on their marriage. No one tells us the complete truth, either. It's like the having-a-baby secret. Women don't tell each other how painful childbirth really is, because who in their right mind would do it if they knew the truth? Of course, all that hard work, pushing, panting, and sweating, is worth it in the end. The same can be said about moving a marriage.

For the purposes of this book, I've defined a moveable marriage as one that relocates due to an employment opportunity for one of the partners. If it's a move abroad, that working partner is usually the husband; 87% of international transferees are men, 70% of them are married, and 60% of relocated couples travel with their children. Among domestic corporate transferees, 84% are men. Those numbers help explain why, first and foremost, this is a book for women. (Although it won't kill a man if he reads it too.)

EACH CHAPTER OF THIS book examines tensions that may already have been lurking under the surface of your marriage but have now become exaggerated by the stress of dislocation. As a woman following a man's career, you'll find potentially hazardous emotional land mines confronting you on your journey away from home.

Some of the challenges will be familiar, others new. There's the shift in the balance of power in your marriage (not necessarily in your favor) and the role the company often plays in exacerbating your marital stress. The loneliness and isolation of a new city or country can be daunting, and can make you grow needy and more dependent on your spouse. There are the considerable ups and downs of creating a new career or reinventing yourself in a new place; your children's feelings and emotional outbursts about the move; the consequences of a husband's business travels or short-term assignments; and the delicate art of renegotiating money and sex after a move.

As a reporter writing for newspapers and magazines at home and abroad, my beat is global living. I've also written three previous books on the subject. For this book, my self-assigned task has been to research and write a story that has long gone unreported: the very real challenges of mobile marriages. I'm not a marriage counselor, although these pages are filled with advice I've sought from professionals. I won't offer solutions, either, but in the stories told in these pages by other relocating spouses—including me—you'll glean many ideas I hope will work in your own marriage.

In the course of my research, I combed the shelves of libraries and bookshops for anything that might describe the realities of relocation and advise those of us forced to move our marriages. Given this age of globalization and mobility, I expected to find hundreds of titles. I did find numerous books on marriage, and many on relocation, but none that put the two subjects together. Along the way, I found many interesting books about women, relationships, self-esteem, and intimacy that are relevant to relocation, although they weren't written with mobility in mind. I've listed the most useful materials and websites I came across in the Resource Guide at the end of this book.

As part of my research, I designed a survey and circulated it to hundreds of accompanying spouses. I also solicited feedback through my website, *www.expatexpert.com*, and through focus groups I conducted during my international lecture tours. I am deeply indebted to the amazing informal network of spouses worldwide who were anxious to assist me with my project, generously responding to my questions with honesty, insight, and wisdom. All of these women's names have been changed to protect their anonymity.

I USED TO CHEEKILY hang my journalism degree in our bathroom wherever we lived in the world—for all the good that degree did me in gaining employment in countries that expel journalists on a regular basis. But it does give me a significant credential to write this book. I have others.

For the first fifteen years of my marriage, my husband's diplomatic career with the Government of Canada took us to New York (my dream assignment, but only for three brief months), back to headquarters in Ottawa, then on to Bangkok for our first overseas assignment. Three years later, we moved back to government headquarters in Ottawa with our first child— our Bangkok-born daughter, Lilly.

Four years later we relocated again, this time with the

addition of our Ottawa-born son, Jamie, beginning a marathon of short-term moves: to Taipei, Taiwan, for one year for my husband's Mandarin language training; to Beijing, China, for two years following that; back to Ottawa for two years; out to Asia again for two years, this time to Seoul, South Korea; and finally repatriation to Canada. Even then, instead of moving to our home base in Ottawa, we settled in Vancouver, British Columbia, where my husband began a second career as president of a company that markets Canadian education internationally.

Along the way, our marriage has experienced considerable highs and lows, and you'll read about many of them in these pages. *A Moveable Marriage* is as much a memoir as a self-help book. I can't claim my marriage is perfect. No marriage can be. But as of this writing, we have happily survived more than twenty-one years together, which I consider to be my greatest qualification for writing this book. (Not to mention the fact that, whenever I speak about this subject publicly, my husband gives me his full support, even though many of my best lines come at his expense.)

With each of our moves, another piece of the moveable-marriage puzzle would fall into place. I've learned over the years that most of the challenges my husband and I encountered are faced by relocating couples everywhere, of all nationalities. I've also learned that a marriage is forever defined by the ways in which the partners relate to each other before, during, and after the relocation.

IN THE YEAR 2000, I was asked to speak at a conference held in Indianapolis called Families in Global Transition. We're actually becoming a movement now, those of us committed to helping families adjust to relocation around the world. The organizers suggested that, since I had constantly referred to my marriage in my previous books, I should simply talk about marriage full stop. So I did just that. I felt a bit like a comic doing a stand-up routine, albeit one on a very serious subject. But when that first discussion turned boisterous and lively, I realized I had touched a nerve.

My fervent hope is that reading this book will help you to stop fretting about your relocating relationship and start taking charge of it. You can't do so until you understand that, along with the tennis rackets, golf clubs, kitchen gadgets, photo albums and the zillion other mementos of your family life, your marriage itself is also being packed up and moved. Hard work, clear thinking about your own needs, and a willingness to take responsibility for keeping your marriage on track will be required to ensure that a precious relationship doesn't get broken in transit. Remember, the two of you *love* each other. Why else, at the end of the day, would you turn your life upside down?

assessing marriage

moveable marriages 101

In my memory, moving days were like a particularly bad flu. Watching my life being thrown into cardboard cartons made me physically sick. Later, when it became a family of four whose lives were being packed and unpacked over and over again, my symptoms only intensified. It finally dawned on me that it wasn't only objects being moved around. My marriage too was being tossed about like a chair or lamp, but without any bubble wrap to cushion it from relocation bumps or breakage.

The marital relationship, more valuable than any of your possessions, typically journeys in an unprotected fog of exhaustion, its principal guardians two irritable adults sniping at each other over road maps and passports, trying to keep cranky children occupied while they load up cars or airport-bound taxis with mountains of baggage. Perched as the adults are on a precipice of frayed nerves, one good gust of wind (a minor argument over a flight time can do it) is enough to plunge them into a full-blown marital storm. This shouldn't come as a surprise. Would anyone in their right mind let a box of fragile dishes ride on the top of a car without being securely tied down?

As women, we are still raised to be superwoman. So it's only natural that, in a relocation situation, we figure we can do it all: move the house, the kids, the dog, our careers, *and* the relationship without breaking a sweat, feeling blue, or losing an ounce of self-esteem or power in our marriages. Who are we kidding, besides ourselves?

In the black-and-white world of television in the 1960s, the father who knew best returned home at the end of the day to find his wife in the kitchen, wearing a freshly pressed apron over a dress adorned with pearls. Those old shows eerily reflect the new life many contemporary women step into when they become the "accompanying spouse" of a man with a job that moves them to a new place.

When she was still in the safe cocoon of her full-time job and the warm, familiar community of friends and family, a woman might have whined all day that the balance between her work and her home life was off-kilter. It was driving her crazy. Oh, what she wouldn't give for some time off to devote to her family! At first, many women heave a sigh of relief at the idea of an enforced sabbatical, a move to a place where employment for them will be difficult or impossible. But the thrill of actually becoming the stay-at-home mom they thought they wanted to be usually wears off after about forty-eight hours, and many women begin to wish with all their hearts that they could be thrown off-balance again. This is the contradictory world of a woman dealing with a relocation.

Everything that distinguishes you as a woman (career, community, church, friends, extended family) disappears when you move. So does your marriage partner, who sets out every morning into a strange new city to do a strange new job. You, meanwhile, face endless days without structure, no one to call, and nowhere to go. Seeds of resentment are planted almost immediately as the new power structure in the relationship becomes obvious.

With time on your hands, are you being asked by your husband to take his shirts or suits to the cleaners? To wait in for the cable guy, the electrician, or other members of the army of service people who will put your new home together? Many women find this the first of many resentment-filled shocks to come: the realization that once moved, the marriage of equals now has a less-than-equal partner. "Suddenly he had all the important responsibilities and I had the day-to-day nonsense" is the way one wife put it to me.

All things are decidedly *not* equal when a marriage relocates, often beginning with the decision to move in the first place. You're not imagining it if you feel like your needs have just dropped to the bottom of the heap. Some women aren't aware of exactly when this shift in the marriage occurred, but others can pinpoint it to the very minute.

"We were at a cocktail party in Taipei," reported Joanne, a forty-seven-year-old American homemaker living in Beijing. "My husband was working as a reporter. I was still teaching English, and people asked me what I did. They all had big jobs doing things other than teaching English, which was considered the lowest rung on the employment ladder. I remember thinking that everyone was awful, which I know now wasn't about them, but about me feeling 'less' because my husband had risen and I hadn't."

Sue, a thirty-eight-year-old Filipina American, re-called: "There is one particular incident that stands out in my mind. I remember having to wait in line to pay our telephone bill for an hour and fifteen minutes and becoming increasingly frustrated. When my husband came home and we compared our days, it turned out he had had lunch with the American ambassador while I stood in line with the locals to pay the lousy phone bill."

Like an earthquake, a move causes a seismic shift in the balance of a marriage. Someone—and that would be you, the wife—is giving up everything familiar to nurture a husband taking a new job elsewhere. The burden of the move (not only the packing, but most of the major adjustments) rests on the woman's shoulders.

By tradition, looking after the emotional well-being of a marriage falls within the woman's domain, so it's no wonder the sizeable job of keeping a moveable marriage intact defaults to the wife. How easy is it, though, to nurture a relationship when your partner is caught up in his new job and just wants you to "Pull yourself together!" and love the new place immediately? Can't he see that something is wrong in the marriage? (Not that he's devoting any time to it, or to you.)

The only way to regain equilibrium in the relationship is by learning new ways to assert yourself. But most women don't find this a simple matter. We're too often suffering from a lack of self-esteem and self-confidence.

As women, we've been struggling with our own self-worth, inside and outside relationships, ever since the first cave*man* started putting up crude drawings that cave*women* desperately tried to live up to. A woman with low self-esteem is going to have a rough time when her community and support are taken away from her. The only person she can rely on to remind her of who she is (her husband) either isn't around, is too preoccupied with his own self-worth to bother with hers, or is sick of talking about the subject.

As the marriage balance begins to tilt like a playground seesaw, a woman's feelings about herself will also swing precipitously, changing with the day, even the hour. Those feelings will definitely find expression with the only person she may know in her new location—her spouse. Even the world's best husband (and mine has scored some pretty impressive marks over the years) isn't saintly enough to be sensitive 365 days of the year. And so the wife's self-esteem challenges, exaggerated by the move, will impact heavily on her relationship until the day life returns to some semblance of order.

Low self-esteem can also make it difficult for women to know what they want out of life. "One should find themselves before moving for one's spouse," wrote late-twenty-something Eleanor, and many other women I heard from agree. In the midst of Eleanor's move, which came at the beginning of her marriage, she confessed: "I have no idea who I am right now. I wish that I had had the sense to figure it out before committing to such a challenging experience." She admitted she was extremely depressed, and while she hoped to snap out of it and not break her husband's heart by ending the relationship, "Given the chance to decide again, I would not have made the choice to move or get married."

A SUCCESSFUL MOVEABLE MARRIAGE is hard work, but how can that work even begin when most couples haven't given much thought to the impact of the move in the first place?

Dixie Wilson of the Houston-based energy giant ConocoPhillips believes couples don't think about it because they don't *get* it. As a member of the company's Employee Assistance Program, interviewing and assessing couples before they leave on assignment is part of her job.

"Before they relocate, couples tend to focus on the externals like where they will live, what schools their children will attend, or where they will buy groceries," says Wilson. "They entirely ignore the internal challenges, so many of which are key to the successful relocation of a relationship. They are in complete denial about the changes which lie ahead for their marriage." Wilson feels a renegotiation of the marriage agreement needs to be undertaken if a couple is going to understand each other in a relocation situation.

For example, from a working spouse's perspective, the pressure on the nonworking spouse in a new city or country can appear minimal because it is often attached to small things.

"The disorienting and isolating feelings are usually brought to light by something like a woman not being able to find a mop in a new city, or even knowing what store would sell one, or how to get there or how to ask for it," says therapist Phyllis Adler. "The lack of control and power this represents is not easily conveyed by the telling of the story itself. It can appear tedious and boring to the husband, who is busy trying to reorganize a multimillion-dollar division of his company."

The situation is much worse, according to Adler, when

the two people have had no experience of moving and so have not done any preparation. In that case, she says, the couple may not be aware of what they are feeling, beyond increased levels of confusion and discomfort. Relationships are not "manageable" in the way companies are manageable. A marriage can't operate like a business, although some couples have successfully adapted corporate tools into their relationships.

Martha, for instance, decided to speak to her husband about their move and its impact in the only language he could understand, that of business. She had moved from the United States to Latin America with kids and a corporate husband who worked in one town while the family lived in another. Martha learned to successfully negotiate her needs using nonemotional, matter-of-fact, case-in-point scenarios. "I did everything short of break out an overhead projector and flowchart!" she said.

Once Martha came across the definition of the word "corporate" ("to make into a body; united; combined"), she never looked back. "By definition, marriage is a corporation. How well is your corporation being run? Who's running the corporation? Do you have a corporate objective? What about benefits, profit sharing, retirement? Name all the positions you maintain within the corporation and be prepared to justify those roles," she advises other spouses. "I've quit more than a few jobs within our corporation, and I've also been asked to resign a few!"

Whether or not using corporate language will work in another woman's marriage is beside the point. Martha and her husband have come up with a new way to communicate that works for them, and you and your partner may need to do that too.

IDEALLY, A MOVE SHOULD be discussed in all its permutations long before the packers turn up at the door, and it's healthier for the marriage if the move is discussed in a nonconfrontational, noncritical way. Over the years, I've learned there is an entire relocation lexicon as well as a certain tone of voice to avoid. My partner's frustration with his government bosses was always triggered when I asked, "When will we know the date we are moving?" That was only marginally better than the dreaded "When will our shipment arrive?" Both questions were a surefire way to drive him nuts, and I admit it: if I was having a bad day and wanted to push his buttons, I would haul out one of those questions from my arsenal and throw it at him.

Sometimes, conversations that start out as mere exchanges of practical information can turn into mudslinging battles for the moral high ground. But there can be no easy victories without damaging the relationship. *Both* partners have a stake in the relocation, and you need to be prepared to approach the move that way.

From your end of things, never assume your spouse is a mind reader. If you have a concern, you need to say so directly and without personal criticism—a theme I will return to many times in this book. Remember, *how* you say what's on your mind is every bit as important as *what* you say.

Often, there's an awful lot your husband is *not* saying, and that's another aspect of the power shift. Lying by omission may not be a mortal sin, but there's a good chance your partner will be avoiding certain subjects.

Just as women nurture the marital relationship by wanting to talk about *everything,* men (not all, but most) usually go into self-defense mode and avoid talking about *anything* to do with the marriage, and that includes any details about the move that could potentially throw the marriage into conflict. My husband, for instance, chose not to tell me before our first diplomatic assignment that I could sign up for an advance workshop called How to Set a Table for Twelve. He wouldn't have dared!

How were you told about your forthcoming move? When a woman feels coerced into a move, or says yes when she really means no, things can get off to a rocky start. Were you consulted, or was your husband's new job a done deal before you realized it? Many women feel they had no power in the decision to make the move in the first place.

Women receive the news of a move in a variety of ways. They usually know something is up. Hints are dropped. A partner is distracted. In the pre-Internet days, an atlas might be yanked off the shelf for no apparent reason and left open in some strategic place, like on the spouse's bedroom pillow. These days, a website bookmarked on the family computer is a dead giveaway. Often, the news comes in a telephone call after your husband has had a long lunch with a vice-president visiting from out of town.

Even when we are *consulted,* it can be in a backhanded way. Before my family went on our final diplomatic posting, my partner played a hypothetical game with me: "What if we were asked to move to Seoul?" Since

(a) I had no idea he was suggesting anything remotely possible (what were the chances, I thought, after we'd already lived in three Asian capitals, of being assigned to a fourth?); and (b) we were on holiday in the Bahamas, with our conversation and stress levels loosened with good Scotch and lots of golf, I was completely cavalier and open about the possibility.

It was only as we were driving to the local airport to pick up my father, flying over to join us for a few days from Florida—to be precise, not until my father had actually stepped off the plane and I was about to shout my greeting—that my husband turned to me and said, "Seoul is not hypothetical. I was offered a job there before we left on holiday, and we'll have to give them a decision when we get back." By way of ending the conversation, he turned to greet my father. I wanted to club my husband over the head with my father's golf clubs as we loaded them into the car. I felt powerless to stop the move, and it hadn't even been officially decided yet. Or had it?

If you are told point-blank by your husband that a job has been offered and already accepted by him, and that's more or less the end of the discussion, the negative aspects of the move will naturally loom much larger. Of course, a lot will also depend on whether mobility is already a part of your marriage.

Couples in which one partner is a military or government service employee, and others who sign on for rotational lives, will make many moves throughout the life of their marriages. They know the score, and experience has taught them how to make the best of the situation. They can anticipate the bumps in the road (even when hit again and again) and are equally aware that these can and will be overcome. Other couples may move once and fly totally blind, only to end up having an experience that will change them, their children, and their relationship for the better.

First moves are like falling in love for the first time. Before leaving, you walk around in a daze, alternating between euphoria and excitement (depending on the destination) or depression and despair, particularly if you have a wonderful job you'll have to leave behind. Distraction and an inability to focus are constant. All those great unknowns can be very frightening.

On top of everything else, there's your relationship. Is your partner supporting you through your dark moments? Is he reassuring you he'll do his best to help you find a job in the new location or supporting your decision to take no job if that's what you want? Or is your husband impatient with your mood swings, angry that you are feeling indecisive? Is he warning you that you won't be seeing him for a few months, because he'll be going on ahead and you'll have to sell and pack up the house, and even once you're there he'll be working 24/7 and there's a heap of travel involved too?

Should you say no to a move? *Can* you? The ability to say no is something many women need to work at, but it's a crucial skill to acquire if you're going to have equal power in your relationship. In a relocation situation, there are many complicating factors. For instance, are you afraid to say no to a move because you think your husband's employer will screw him if he turns it down? Do you think the move will be bad for your kids?

Saying no has never been my strong point. When my partner finally decided to leave the foreign service for the private sector, he came home yet again with *great news!* He had a terrific job offer in Vancouver. A beautiful city on Canada's West Coast, Vancouver is a fantastic tourist destination, but it seemed to me to be an insular, parochial place, sheltered from the rest of the world behind mountains, and it was very far from my family and friends in Central and Eastern Canada. I didn't want to move there. I vividly remember sitting on our bed, screaming inside my head: *Say no!* Instead, I smiled sweetly and said how great it would be for all of us.

It took about three years for the terrific part to begin, and I certainly didn't have a crystal ball handy at the time to let me see into our future. In hindsight, I know I should have been up front about my feelings, because it affected the way we settled into Vancouver. I clearly didn't want to be there, and my husband was away on business before the paint had dried on our new house. My inability to voice my feelings contributed to a rocky relocation of our relationship. Fortunately, we soldiered on, but I have made it perfectly clear that there will be no next time.

WHETHER THIS IS YOUR first move as a couple, or you are a rotational family and this is your third move in five years, it's important to notice how the move is being presented. For example, do you feel you have any say whatsoever in the destination?

Sometimes, an employee himself is given no choice. "You're going to Timbuktu and that's it!" says the company. The military also regularly uproots its personnel and families and sends them to live on another base, whether in their home country or overseas. But sometimes an organization allows room for maneuvering or offers a choice of destinations, and sometimes one of those options may even *appeal* to you. Find out if your husband has a say in the matter, and be advised that sometimes you might have to force him to ask his company or organization.

At the same time, find out if you are allowed to talk about the impending move with anyone other than your husband. If you want your marriage to stay on track during the often crazy period when you're waiting to hear the final details, and your partner is telling you to sit on the news, my advice is to negotiate the right to designate one discreet person who can be let in on the secret. Keeping your feelings inside, letting them out only when your partner comes home yet again with no news, is bad for the marriage. Nor is it great if he takes all the power of "telling" and leaves you with none. You are *both* moving, and it is no small incident in your life. It's amazing how much pressure is released by this small concession. Here are some other ways to share power in the marriage during this period.

Negotiate the tasks

Many women are left behind by a working spouse who goes on ahead, often by months, to the new destination. They must put a house on the market, clean and pack it for the movers, and look after all of the children's leave-takings and emotional crises. As a result, the relationship is off-balance right from the beginning. At least, that's the way it looks from your perspective. I spoke about this once to an audience of women (and a few men) in London. One couple perfectly illustrated the different points of view: the wife claimed to have done 99% of the move, because she'd been responsible for all the domestic tasks, while her husband felt *he* had done most of the work, because of all the financial and other strategic matters that *he* had attended to. Regardless of how you see the picture, make sure you're both seeing the same one by making a giant to-do list that spells out *all* of the tasks associated with a relocation. Surprisingly, it may turn out that the responsibilities are more or less evenly split.

Negotiation will be an ongoing process. At first, you're involved in a major overhaul, figuring out how the power in the marriage will be shared given the new circumstances. Later, negotiating sessions will provide you with a road map for keeping balances and checks in place. When couples are accustomed to sharing the power in decisions on everything from home renovations to a child's education, it can be a significant shock upon moving if one partner (your husband) suddenly has the power of Zeus and is making all the decisions because he is the only one with the information or because he has decided that, as the sole breadwinner in your new location, it's his right. At the end of the day, renegotiating ways that power can be shared is one key to restoring mutual respect.

It's true what they say about power: it's often harder to relinquish than to exercise. When you *both* decide who will do what—without one person feeling hard done by—your marriage is on the road to success.

Think like a team

The most successful couples operate as a team. Melanie

and her husband, Bob, relocated to Europe for his job, a move they'd been trying to figure out how to make since their first trip to the continent in 1987.

"We decided that there was a lot to see in the world, and if we lived overseas, we'd be able to explore more of it," said Melanie, whose professional career in a variety of occupations never offered a management track that included reassignments. For ten years of their marriage, she was the breadwinner. Then Bob took a job in the corporate world that led them to his new overseas assignment.

"He knew he was exchanging his autonomy for company politics, but it was in the interest of pursuing our *joint* goal of living overseas," Melanie said. "What each of us brings to the mix changes from year to year, but we definitely try to be a team."

And a team sticks together through thick and thin.

Sit down with your partner to ask one another about individual goals and to set common objectives for yourselves as a couple or perhaps as a family. Listening to each other's hopes and dreams can be a positive experience if you create a sense that you're both working towards the same end *and* want to support the other in achieving his or her goals.

When we lived in Taipei, it was my husband's goal to complete enough Mandarin language training to work in Beijing. My goal was to complete a draft of my first-ever manuscript. I had the lion's share of responsibility for our children, but there were days when my husband took over, writing out complex Chinese characters while our son played with Lego beside him on our bed so that

I could sit quietly and work on my book. We supported each other's goals—successfully—and that went a long way towards helping our marriage survive its most difficult year.

Regularly engage in "end of the day" conversations

Couples can share power in their marriage by <u>reconnecting with one another</u> as often as possible during the disconnecting experience of relocation. Think of this time as the "team meeting." You and your partner can sit down and share both the pressures and the excitement that the day has brought. The key here is in the *listening*. Whether you want the adjective in front of that verb to be *active* or *supportive* (I've heard therapists use both), the key is for each of you to listen as your partner rants and raves.

Pick a time that's suitable for your family. (Obviously, parents of small children can't speak the minute the father walks in the door.) These conversations will help you and your partner feel connected to each other. The more connected you feel, the less inclined you will be to fight over the small stuff. So often, in the overwhelming process of moving, couples aren't aware that an "emotional disconnect" is building a wall that will grow higher with each passing day if neither partner attempts to scale it.

Get your husband to tell you about the characters in his office. Likewise, describe the eccentric or colorful characters you met that day or the trouble you had finding your way to the grocery store. These conversations will allow you to entertain each other, blow off steam, bring the other partner into your loop—all with the goal of giving each other whatever is needed: support, sympathy, or just a big hug.

Best-selling marriage guru Dr. John Gottman writes in *The Seven Principles for Making Marriage Work*: "Happily married couples aren't smarter, richer or more psychologically astute than others. But in their day-to-day lives, they have hit upon a dynamic that keeps their negative thoughts and feelings about each other (which all couples have) from overwhelming their positive ones." Dr. Gottman calls this dynamic "emotional intelligence."

In order to restore and maintain marital balance when a relationship moves, being smart and knowledgeable about the emotional part of the relocation—all the ups and downs, external vs internal challenges, positives vs negatives—is clearly required.

If you are hesitating about a move or feeling uncertain of yourself because it's still early days, sometimes you need to realize it's simply a natural fear of the unknown that's making you feel crazy. And sometimes, that unknown factor amazingly vanishes once you settle in at your new destination. You may surprise yourself (and look back on it all later with amusement) as you recall how you almost didn't move to a place that turned out to be the greatest experience of your life.

the role of the company

I'm going to cut straight to the bottom line (pun intended) in my discussion of companies and the moveable marriage.

Most businesses and organizations that relocate employees can take credit for creating or magnifying the major challenges of moveable marriages. Widespread corporate indifference, combined with an appalling lack of coherent family relocation policies, is directly responsible for the breakdown of marriages and for numerous relationship problems, often requiring extensive marriage or family counseling to rectify. Organizational behavior regarding family relocation in general, and marriage in particular, often borders on immorality. The neglect is heartless at worst, needless at best, and is the result of blatant gender discrimination.

Have I got everyone's attention?

An article that appeared in the *Wall Street Journal* in the early '90s perfectly illustrates my last point. The "news story" was about the fact that more men were becoming relocating spouses and they needed the business world to help them cope. It was as if women, who had been relocating with their partners all these years, didn't exist. Our challenges were not worthy of attention. But now that *men* were being asked to move, there was a sudden interest in the stress of relocating for a spouse. It had become an issue to be taken seriously.

On my speaking tours, I'm constantly being asked by businesspeople about the conditions for trailing male spouses and what can be done to help them. Here's how I respond: although the men's concerns are legitimate (as are those of all spouses), their numbers are insignificant. Focusing on the small male minority only distracts companies from dealing with the majority— female spouses. I don't believe their concerns would even warrant attention if they weren't men. Well over 80% of all business transfers, domestic and international, are made by men, and more than two-thirds of them are married. Half of the remaining small percentage of women who move for their jobs are not married. Do the math.

The reason there's the perception of a greater number of traveling husbands is simply that men, unlike women, aren't afraid to ask for support services. As a result, relocation companies report working more often with men.

Writing about demographic trends in the March 2002 issue of *Mobility*, the official publication of the American Employee Relocation Council, Ed Marshall and Peggy Greenwood reported that an extraordinarily high percentage (almost 40%) of clients receiving services at one American relocation company were male. They explained the huge discrepancy in numbers this way: "One factor may be corporate sensitivity to the perceived need of the accompanying male to be quickly re-employed, resulting in more frequent corporate use of family transition services."

This gender profiling in relocation practices is hardly subtle. In every place I've lived, visited, or contacted, I've heard at least one infuriating story about a male spouse who showed up and was automatically handed a key to the office or had a coveted work permit purchased for him. Many women, meanwhile, continue to be fed platitudes by the company about local labor laws and are rarely subsidized for work permits. Obviously not all male spouses have been treated well, but they are already receiving more attention than their numbers deserve.

THE CEO, PRESIDENT, DIRECTOR, or top dog of any company or organization should take the ultimate blame for breaking up or otherwise harming a transferring employee's marriage. The buck stops and *starts* at the top. And sitting there, 9.99 times out of 10, is a white, gray-haired man in his late fifties or sixties whose own career has benefited from the moves he's made and who firmly believes in the efficacy of mobility because he now sits in the corner office. Today's mobile executive, especially one who has uprooted his family to an overseas locale, is not so lucky.

Consider these statistics from the Center for Global Assignment about what happens when transferred employees move back home from overseas:

- 77% of returning employees take a job at a lower level
- 46% of returning employees have reduced autonomy within the company
- 66% of employers do not guarantee post-assignment positions

- 49% of expatriate executives leave their companies within two years of returning

And, oh yes: 11% of employees advanced their careers because they moved.

Too many companies treat women and children like pieces of luggage. Yet even as baggage handlers, these companies are complete and utter failures. If luggage arrived in the same banged-up shape some families do, there would be a lawsuit seeking compensation for damages. But how can you put a price on a shattered marriage? Even if a spouse were to start a legal challenge, the company would probably be shaking its head trying to figure out who she was, since most companies openly admit they have no database of company spouses.

One corporate spouse in the United States did try—unsuccessfully—to sue her former husband's company, the Whirlpool Corporation, in the '90s. Rosalyn Reeder recounts the circumstances in *Divorcing the Corporation*. It's an amazing tale of broken promises, petty corporate politics, and a marriage of thirty-eight years that ended in divorce. Although Reeder's story hit a nerve with a number of Whirlpool employees, according to the author, the case never made it to court. Her all-too-common horror story, which involved a miserable, failed relocation to Brazil (one she'd never wanted, as she'd told the company on countless occasions), was at the end of the legal day interpreted as just the way corporate America does business.

Reeder's now a seventy-two-year-old grandmother, still living in St. Joseph, Michigan, a company town of twenty thousand and headquarters for Whirlpool. Her story is dramatic enough to have piqued the interest of actress Anne Bancroft, since Reeder's ex-husband, besides being a loyal company man, grew up in Nazi Germany and was actually a member of the Nazi party. In her book, Reeder doesn't flinch from describing the corporate tactics used to get her to go to Brazil as "fascist." Her former husband, meanwhile, lives with a second wife in New Mexico.

Reaction to Reeder's book in the company town was a mixture of denial—on the part of the company's corporate executives—and gratitude from many company employees for exposing what they saw as the truth about corporate immorality. "The local bookstore got a call from an eager company human resource type who wanted to buy up all the copies," Reeder told me. "Fortunately, the bookshop owner said there were more where those came from!"

Most of the appalling company stories I've received from accompanying spouses through my website echo the charges of underhanded corporate behavior Reeder levels in her book. Here's a small sampling.

"The company did not want me to make our move in the first place and gave me no support, no visa, nothing at all. My husband seemed to take that lack of support as a cue to all but ignore my feelings about the whole issue, as well as my unhappiness about not being able to find work or satisfaction in our present location."

"In my husband's company, wives and family come at the bottom of the list. In all of my locations, I have never once had any help settling in. I'm dropped in and have to find my own way while my husband is snowed down in work for the first twelve months in each location."

"The home office is out of touch with reality. There is the occasional foray into our world, where they hole up in the security of the local five-star hotel and stay there for all of their meetings. There is no support there."

DEPENDENTS DESPERATELY NEED SUPPORT, but it's an expensive anathema to CEOs who have no problem paying themselves multimillion-dollar salaries and stock options (even when the company is losing money) but use fiscal losses to explain why "soft" training programs must be eliminated for the sake of the shareholder. In a post-Enron era in which "infectious greed" has finally been exposed, the lip service the business world pays to the importance of its so-called human capital is particularly obscene.

Older CEOs were married and traveling long before dual career families were the norm. They earned something once quaintly called a "family wage," enough for a family of four to live on, so the dual career issue was a nonstarter. Moreover, they didn't live in a high-tech age that has had the contradictory impact of keeping people in touch over long distances but isolating them desperately when they move to new communities where people e-mail their neighbors. Try making new friends with people too busy to see their old ones.

In my perfect relocation fantasy world, the CEO is a man who has moved many times for his career. Along the way, his wife has had a nervous breakdown, developed a drinking problem, or starting screwing around on him from sheer loneliness in her road-warrior widowhood. His children have either run away from home or tried to kill themselves over the stress of growing up fatherless while moving so often. Now *that's* a CEO who will approve funding to implement company change in support of family, because he has felt the pain personally.

Management demographics are changing, but the mentality fostered by these old men is not adapting fast enough. Let's face it: what guy can resist the initial idea of having a wife at home doing nothing but ironing his shirts and looking after his children? It's tempting, to be sure, but most men of the twenty-first century are way past that kind of thinking, even if they require a nudge to get there.

So although you will never change the dinosaur CEO's mind, you *can* change your husband's, and that's where you should concentrate your efforts if you want to preserve your marriage. After all, you already have his heart.

WHEN MY FIRST BOOK, *Culture Shock! Successful Living Abroad: A Wife's Guide*, was published, I received a variety of reactions from women in response to my lifting the veil of silence that, by unspoken tradition, had settled over the effects of culture shock on a traveling wife. While most applauded my honesty and found my words comforting or inspirational, not everyone agreed with me. I didn't expect universal agreement, naturally, for what a boring world it would be if we all saw things the same way. However, when a woman would tell me, with a straight face, that she had never for one minute experienced the shock of a relocation, that life had been smooth sailing, her marriage was absolutely hunky-dory, and that was only her third gin and tonic in her hand, here's what I would say: "How lucky for you! I hope you are sharing your good fortune by helping someone who is less fortunate and having a tough time adjusting to her move."

My position remains firm: if your partner's company is in that very small group of enlightened organizations, share your support stories! Spread the enlightenment! As will become evident in these pages, women so often don't know what to ask for by way of support or compensation. Your experiences can help others receive similar moral bounty. And don't for an instant forget to be grateful about your own situation.

mind vs. heart

ON THE PRACTICAL LEVEL, there are basic things you need to know about company behavior if you want to avoid conflict with your husband.

- First of all, you need to rid yourself from the get-go of any expectations of help from the company transferring your spouse. If you do get help, usually only after bugging your partner to ask for it, consider it a bonus.
- If you're thinking of trying to communicate with the company directly over a move, save your breath. Human Resources departments *hate* speaking directly to the spouse and will avoid it at all costs. They will communicate only through your mouthpiece, your husband. Phone calls or e-mails from you will usually not be answered. Be prepared to argue with your husband about this. And bear in mind that often he doesn't want you communicating with the office, either—who knows what you will say? (Shall I ask my husband to step in here and relate *his* horror stories about *me?*)
- Your move will probably be farmed out to a relocation

company paid by the corporation. Not to say there aren't some wonderful and capable relocation companies out there, but remember who pays their bills. Their clients often measure a relocation company's success by its ability to reduce the cost of a relocation.

- You will become an unpaid relocation consultant yourself. I used to love it when someone would say to me before a move, "You have movers, so what's the big deal?" Moving companies don't sort through your house, give away half of what's inside, clean it up, pack up everyone's stuff, or decide what goes or stays. You'll have to do that, as well as write up an inventory of everything you own, especially what's being left behind in storage. When you arrive somewhere new, it will likely be another company spouse who shows you around. Take notes, because you will be doing it yourself one day—for free, of course.

- The information provided by the Human Resources department will focus almost exclusively on tax issues or compensation and benefits. An accompanying spouse is rarely, if ever, involved in these financial discussions with the company.

- Finally, expect broken company promises on everything from work permits to holidays to housing. The company wants your husband in the job yesterday and will say anything to get him there. (And once there, expect him to be sent out of town on the day the movers arrive and you start to unpack.)

Remember, only *you* have the power to make sure the company's neglect doesn't crush your self-esteem by making you feel you aren't worth the price of one day's travel by an executive vice-president on the corporate jet. Start believing you *are* worth it, and keep reading.

FROM THE MOMENT YOUR husband is called into a meeting to discuss a relocation, the company has created a dangerous dynamic in the marriage. He is now at the mercy of his employer, and you are now totally reliant on him to convey the information and all the downstream effects of the move. Want to eavesdrop on that meeting?

Manager A has a meeting with Human Resources to discuss an international assignment. Turns out the place the company has selected is the worst possible place for a spouse or family. (For a variety of reasons: political unrest, environmental danger, less than zero chance of a spouse working. Pick one.)

Being a devoted husband and father, Manager A replies honestly (this is supposed to be an exploratory meeting, after all) that the suggested relocation won't work for his family. Is there anywhere else he might be needed?

"Oh," says the HR manager. "That's too bad about your spouse. I see your point." A polite beat skips by. "Will you go alone?"

"No, I won't go alone," responds Manager A. "I don't want to break up my family. I guess we'll just stay put for now."

"Hmmm," says the HR manager, "if that's what you prefer. . ." She leaves the comment hanging.

Sensing something isn't right, Manager A then asks, "That *will* be all right, won't it? I can stay where I am? I won't risk my career and future promotions, will I?"

"Oh," says the HR manager. "Of course you'll be all right. I think. Yes, I'm sure we can find *something* for you to do here at headquarters. Probably won't be the same as you have now."

They stare at each for a few minutes. Finally, the HR manager speaks as if a lightbulb has suddenly gone on above her head. (Take a look at a photograph of international HR managers and note the high number of women. Human Resources, after all, remains a powerless and thankless company function, outside the strategic loop of the company since the department doesn't make money, it *spends* it.)

"Would it be helpful if this was a short-term assignment?" she asks. That was likely the intent all along, since short-term assignments are the new HR magic bullet, capable of stopping accompanying spousal concerns dead in their tracks. (More on that in chapter 7.)

"That depends," says Manager A, wanting to appear flexible. "How long do you think you would need me for?"

"Oh, probably only three months. To begin with."

"What do you mean, 'to begin with'?"

"It may end up being longer, but look at it this way: at least your wife doesn't have to live there."

"When do you want me to start?" the manager is none too subtly coerced into asking, all the while wondering how the heck he's going to take this news home with him. Being a nice guy, he probably told his wife he was having a meeting that day, and she'll be waiting to hear all about it.

"By the way," adds the HR person as the manager rises to leave, "keep this to yourself for now. I wouldn't tell your wife about it until we know something for sure."

And that's how the employee finds himself stuck between that proverbial rock (the company) and a hard place (the spouse). All of this happens because he is concerned the assignment will kill his family if he says yes and kill his career if he says no. Even going for an indefinite, open-ended "short term" might kill his marriage, if he isn't murdered first in his sleep by his wife once she learns how long he has known about the possibility of reassignment and not informed her.

When your husband finally can speak openly about the job offer and relate the conversations he's had with his superiors, you realize the company has thrown you, the wife, into a no-win situation. You will feel, as many women have told me over the years, that if you don't agree to the move, it will adversely affect your husband's career and most certainly damage your relationship.

"It's about having no control," Marg, a fifty-something high-tech wife married for more than twenty years, wrote to me. "It's about having no control over where I live. I'm tired of being the limb that bends."

WHEN MY HUSBAND FIRST became a foreign service officer, I remember being at a party and overhearing one of his new colleagues relate what he thought was an extremely funny story about someone else's spouse.

"Imagine," this fellow was saying, as if the world had turned humorously upside down. "So-and-so's wife *insisted* on being at the meeting with Personnel. Can you imagine anything so crazy? Boy, that guy is really going to have trouble."

"Why is that?" I asked, poking my head into the conversation. (Demonstrating, I suppose, that I was a rabble-rouser from the beginning.)

The man turned to me with one of those withering, patronizing looks many spouses have come to expect from company officials but don't anticipate will come from someone also in "the life."

"Well, what does *she* have to do with the assignment, anyway? It's *his* job," he finally responded.

I lost my cool, of course. My sympathy for this guy's wife (boy, I thought, *he's* the one who's going to have trouble unless he changes his attitude) contributed to my outrage. I gave the partygoer a strongly worded piece of my mind. The words "the entire family is being moved" probably still reverberate in his head.

The spouse must be privy to *all* the available information, including where exactly the family is moving, when they are moving (does it coincide with the school schedule?), and what, if anything, the company will be doing to support her. When she is not given all the information, when she is excluded from the negotiations, she becomes vulnerable and can be easily manipulated by both her husband and his company.

Relocation takes traditional marriages (that is, husband as breadwinner, wife at home raising kids) to an entirely new level. Trust and love aside for a minute (yes, I do believe in those two virtues), women are extremely vulnerable in a marriage once they give up their place in the workforce and can't make money. And all the inherent vulnerabilities of the marriage itself are now exaggerated by a relocation.

By excluding the spouse from the discussion, the corporation paints a false family portrait. The company's indifference to (and ongoing dismissal of) the needs of the accompanying spouse doesn't acknowledge her prominence in the picture or how indispensable she is to the entire relocation scenario. Perhaps a halo over her head is a bit of a stretch, but a wife's face should be bathed in white light, for it is she who nurtures the employee so he can do his job well and make money for the company.

The ever-pragmatic British recognized this early in their colonial days. The British East India Company was a pioneer of the modern-day company-sponsored relocated lifestyle. It introduced the idea of sending an employee's spouse to its far-flung empires. The firm felt that a spouse's calming influence would help reduce employee turnover, increase efficiency, and breed loyalty to the company. The spouse apparently would also act as a civilizing force on too many employees who were going "native," a situation frowned upon by the colonials.

Women are "in the service" of their husband's career (and indirectly in the service of the company) by allowing their mate to meet his need for "sustained achievement drive." Research by sociologist Martha R. Fowlkes, which appeared in an enlightening paper published in *Employment and Family Life Journal,* makes this point clearly: "Successful male professional careers are propped up at every turn by the roles of the wives of professional men." Contributing to his career is one thing, but wives also contribute to his productivity.

When company executives ignore the needs of the spouse, as I tell corporate audiences at every opportunity, they are doing so at their financial peril. A man can't work effectively if he's being hassled all day long by his wife at home threatening to slit her wrists over a moving company's inability to deliver the family's goods intact. (Shall I call upon my husband to interject again here?) More important to the subject at hand, if the husband has been bothered all day by distraught telephone calls because no one is helping his wife, how do you think that couple is going to meet up at the end of the day? In an atmosphere of mutual respect? As if. When companies want their employees to perform well, they have to make it easier for the wife to do her job (unpaid as it is) in equal measure.

ENLIGHTENED COMPANIES INTERESTED IN maintaining a mentally healthy workforce have, among other initiatives, established Employee Assistance Programs (EAPs) or, in the case of the armed forces, Military Family Support Centers. Some companies contract out employee support to a growing number of psychological service groups. Trained counselors speak confidentially to employees about stressful subjects that may be distracting them from their work. Marriage counseling is a large part of what these professionals offer. If you find as a couple that you need an outside facilitator to help you work through the burning issues and challenges of a pending move, get yourself signed up for a few sessions if you can.

Sometimes in the corporate world, counselors are also used to administer "assessment tools" designed to evaluate if potentially relocating couples have the "right stuff," especially for an overseas assignment. Questions are asked to measure flexibility, ability to adapt to change, tolerance for other cultures, and any number of other factors that can affect whether the assignment will succeed.

"An assessment helps couples examine their personal and relationship styles in terms of the stresses of making a move, especially an international one. It helps them see and decide for themselves not only if they can handle the move, but w<u>hat challenges they will face</u>," says therapist Dr. Jill Kristal, who has worked with relocated couples in London, England. "Ideally, the assessment should be one component among many related to relocation adjustment. In <u>a perfect world</u>, the couple should examine their relationship prior to the decision to accept the transfer, but during a predeparture assessment they can also be helped to develop skills to cope with the change."

Pre-assessments, though, can be both good news and a bad-news joke. The good news first. If questions are answered honestly, couples who have issues that will truly make a move difficult will be weeded out of the process early on, saving both the company and the family a lot of grief.

Now the bad news. As in any other situation engineered by the employer, what people say could possibly have an impact on the career of the employee being transferred. As a result, a couple may not be completely forthright in the assessment exercises or the interviews that go with them. They worry, rightly or wrongly, that information may be held against them or that domestic issues they'd prefer to keep private will become part of the company's database.

Sally Lipscomb, a Chicago-based EAP specialist who has been an accompanying spouse herself, says the assessment procedure can help couples if they are completely frank with the counselor doing the assessing. But first, she warns, couples should negotiate in writing some "rules of release" for the information they provide.

"Couples should pay close attention to the agreement covering the release of any information gathered in this process," says Lipscomb. "Find out exactly what that release is and, at the same time, establish some measure of trust with the counselor, even if that trust cannot be written down. If you know what the rules are and feel confident they will be followed, the pre-assessment can be a wonderful opportunity for couples to sort out some of the pre-existing difficulties in the marriage that will prove troublesome later."

In other words: exercise caution, but if it's offered, don't waste the opportunity to work with a professional who may play a very helpful role in determining the state of your marriage and, ultimately, how your relationship dynamics will play out during a stressful relocation.

SOMETIMES, WOMEN NEED TO seek professional help on their own to sort through ambivalent emotions. How do you really feel about moving and re-creating a life without your regular support system? Happy? Sad? Excited? Depressed? Overwhelmed? Angry? Resentful? These are just a few of the reactions women expressed to me in my survey and in conversations. In the face of an impending move, many spouses keep themselves so busy they are numb with exhaustion at the end of the day, unable to think about anything other than pack-up dates, obtaining kids' school or dental records, or squeezing in a few final visits with friends.

When bedtime arrives, some couples are so excited about their move they have no problem connecting with each other. But there are many others who say, as I know I did, "Are you out of your mind? You think I want sex right *now?*"

Ambivalence plunks itself right there on the marriage bed. A woman might have worked up a good sweat ranting about the company for the entire evening (because it's safer to get exorcized about an institution than about her husband). When it's time to turn in, she's anything but turned on to the idea of marital relations. She's feeling way too conflicted about her partner and the way his company is treating her during the relocation.

So much heartache over relocation springs from our guilty feelings—sometimes buried, other times close to the surface—towards our husbands. We *want* to support them and their careers, but wonder why it's always *their* lives and *their* careers that get the attention. At the same time, we're ashamed of ourselves for feeling this way about someone we love, someone who's a terrific father and a wonderful husband who's treated us well.

Other women feel guilty about somehow "letting down the side" when they realize they don't want to work anymore, and now they have a tremendous excuse not to. Or that finally they can get away from that bitch who lives around the corner! For myself, I know I can sometimes be drowning in the guilt of my own ambivalence but still be damned if I'm going to say so. It's always easier to keep blasting other people, especially my husband and his employer.

I know these are all common feelings, because so many women have shared them with me. So you are certainly not alone. The trouble begins when you try to *deny* that those feelings exist, to insist on putting on a happy face all the time when nobody is that perfect or, worse, transfer your personal responsibility for your own well-being onto the nearest target at hand, whether it be the corporation, your husband, or your children. This is *your* issue to resolve. Many women do not want to face it. It's simply too painful.

But sooner or later you have to snap out of it. I have little sympathy for women who deny their feelings and then turn the relocation experience into an opportunity to be a victim or martyr. It's very easy to blame others for the choices you make. But ultimately you do choose whether or not to move of your own free will, and if you make a bad choice, it's no one's fault but your own.

In times of transition and change, a woman must be prepared to do the inner work to know herself: not only what she wants and needs, but her own limitations and flaws, so that these don't throw a smoke screen of discontent around the entire family during a relocation. It's difficult and often disturbing work, but ambivalence is hard enough in any marriage, and it puts an extraspecial strain on a mobile one. For the sake of her marriage and herself, a woman must stop blaming everyone in her path (husband, company, kids, society) and take responsibility for her life. If she can't do it on her own, well then, that's why psychologists were invented.

As women, we so often don't get what we want or need in relationships because we don't ask. The happiest couples I've seen or spoken to are those in which the woman has acquired the ability to negotiate for her needs and thus balance out her relationship. In my own case, the moment I took control of my fate and worked to make new situations good for me, I improved my marriage immeasurably. I wasn't lying around depressed all day, feeling sorry for myself and blaming *him* for everything.

One way to begin the process is to avoid being your own worst enemy. Quit whining, as I did, out of one side of your mouth while the other side smiles sweetly and says "Yes, dear" to everything related to the move. We all want to be sensitive and loving partners to a man facing challenges of his own in a new corporate culture or workplace, but it doesn't have to be at the expense of our own needs.

By the time you finish reading this book, I hope you will have learned some new strategies for taking charge of your position in the relationship, for proactively making your marriage and your life the best they can be.

To create win-win scenarios involving you (the spouse), your husband (the employee), and the company honchos you're dealing with, you'll need a strategy that covers these three relevant points in that triangular relationship. Begin with the most important relationship, that between you and your husband. To avoid making matters more tense in the marriage, consider establishing some unofficial ground rules.

Set up a special time and place to discuss moving matters

Before a move, I used to hit my husband in the eye, literally, with my questions the moment he walked in the door from work. Wrong strategy! He was busy trying to figure out his own career logistics, and so my approach of knocking him over with questions or complaints before he had even taken his coat off did not set the scene for constructive discussions.

44

Designate a time and place to talk about the potential fallout from a move. Limit these "meetings" to a certain amount of time, then go for a walk afterwards or arrange to do something pleasurable. Otherwise, you can get caught in a terrible nonstop cycle of complaining, leading to anger and resentment on both sides.

Make a list of what needs to be negotiated

To avoid fights, decide between you what is absolutely vital. For instance, if your parents are elderly and will want their daughter (that's you!) home as much as possible, find out in advance how many trips back to your home turf the company will pay for. Then get the company to sign an agreement to that effect. That's not to say an agreement can't be broken (I've heard many stories of contractual agreements never met), but the thorny issue of aging parents can really get contentious between a husband and wife. He's working and you're worrying.

Likewise, if children are left behind in boarding school or university, there has to be some agreement about the number of trips back and forth that situation will entail, and how often the company will pay for them. If all of this is talked about in advance and an understanding is reached, there will be less friction between partners, especially if a company reneges.

Recognize your partner's limitations

I didn't harangue corporations earlier in this chapter just to hear the sound of my own voice. If there's a lesson to be learned from what I wrote, it's this: your husband is very likely butting heads with a corporate culture that doesn't want to even hear the word "family."

It really helps if you appreciate and respect that your partner must tread lightly when he raises your concerns, and that his fears of being branded a troublemaker and then watching his career go down the drain are all too realistic. He's not making them up. He'll be more willing to go to bat for you if you acknowledge his worries as well as your own, and trust that he will do what he can. After all, you will have already patiently explained how it's in his best interest to keep you happy as well as the company.

Pick your company fights carefully

Think a moment about what's worth fighting over and what isn't. In my travels, I've met women professionals, for instance, who married rotational employees yet still fully expected they'd be able to carry on as doctors or lawyers or in some other profession requiring language abilities and certification as they moved around. And they expected their husbands to make sure they'd be able to do this. Come on!

Be realistic about what you expect your husband or a company to do for you, and graciously accept what can't be done. In our age of entitlement, it can be difficult to be told no, but some things are just not going to happen. A company may, for instance, have sympathy for a wife leaving behind an elderly parent or a child in boarding school or university and fund some of her visits back home. But be prepared to negotiate some items and let go of others. You won't get everything you want, so save your strength to fight the big battles (perhaps special education for a child) and let the smaller ones go. Showing a willingness to be flexible will win you a lot of points with your husband.

46

A SPOUSE NEEDS TO know what kind of support, if any, her husband's company can potentially offer. Ask other experienced spouses for their advice and read as much as you can about your new destination. *Never* ignore what's being offered, or you'll ruin it for everyone else—if no one takes advantages of services, companies won't continue to extend them. Here are a few reasonable possibilities.

Predeparture look-see visits

Would anyone in their right mind move home and hearth to a new house in a new city without doing a little reconnaissance first? Doubtful. More and more companies are providing for a look-see visit. To make the most of these, leave your children with a grandparent or friends if possible. You can always make a videotape of the location for your children, but you need space as a couple to assess a place for its suitability in the areas of housing, schools, hospitals, and leisure amenities.

If planned right, a look-see can allow a couple the quiet time to take mutual pleasure in their new surroundings or share excitement about an impending move, so make every effort to create a special time for yourselves. Plan a weekend somewhere at the end of the official visit as a way to feel even more closely connected.

Predeparture training

This is one of the "soft" training services I mentioned earlier that may have been cut back, or in which a human trainer has been replaced by a computer, but it's absolutely vital that couples attend anything offered along these lines *together*. (You'd be surprised how often this is made difficult by companies who keep the employee too busy to attend any sessions.) Predeparture training can include everything from practical introductions to a new culture or a new city to language and cross-cultural training. Some really enlightened companies even offer this training to prepare children for the move, so be sure to ask if that's available.

If I had one major reason for writing this book, it's to stress that couples need to think about the impact of relocation on their marriage. In ideal circumstances, this is done as part of predeparture training. If it's not offered formally by the company, then take the initiative and create some form of it yourself with a marriage counselor or company Employee Assistance Program representative.

Carlanne Herzog, an interculturalist and psychologist who also lived as a relocating oil company spouse for more than twenty years, developed "couples training" for marriage partners to take before they leave home. She feels it's critical both partners visualize what lies ahead for the other.

"Most employee spouses never give much thought to what their wife might be going through, but I try to help partners see what challenges lie ahead for both, and guide them to the skills they will need to help one another through their respective challenges," says Herzog. "It's a real eye-opener for most people, especially the husbands. I think of the work I do with couples before they move abroad as an 'equipping' exercise."

Spousal career assistance

This kind of training and consultation, if available, should come both before the move and directly afterwards, as soon as the spouse has her head out of the moving boxes and is ready to consider her next professional step. There is a veritable smorgasbord of career services these days, from cv-writing workshops and actual job searches to companies that will help spouses get a work permit abroad. Find out what the company is offering (especially on the issue of work permit assistance). When promises are made in the latter instance, get them in writing.

I looking at spousal career challenges and their impact on the marriage in chapter 4, but for now, keep in mind that broken company promises over work permits and professional opportunities abound. Try to head off fighting with your spouse about this issue by getting everything promised in writing from day one.

Help on arrival

While it's true that a welcoming brass band would be over-the-top, a company representative or relocation specialist hired by the company in the new location would be a nice gesture and helpful, too, especially in matters of housing. Tension between couples only worsens if, the morning after arrival, the employee is whisked away in a company car from temporary lodgings and the spouse is left alone, or trapped with kids, in a hotel room with no one to talk to all day and likely part of the evening, when the employee is either still working or being taken out for a welcome drink by other staff. Life immediately improves for a spouse when a call comes in from another company spouse or a local relocation service provider. Make sure this service is provided for you. Even the name and address of the local Welcome Wagon will help.

Spousal intranets and connectivity projects

If a spouse wants to be really daring, she can suggest, through the mouthpiece of her husband, of course, that the company consider projects like those that follow.

Some of the greatest company success stories involve using technology to support spouses and help them stay connected with other employees' families. Spouse-Connect, put together by the oil services giant Schlumberger, is a good example of using high tech as a high-touch tool. More than three thousand Schlumberger spouses (the number rises every month) are put in touch with each other through this program. It involves not only an intranet they can access for information about moving details and company programs, but also takes away some of the computer dependence many spouses have on their working mates. Spouses are trained to help each other find their way around the net and get e-mail accounts sorted out when new families arrive.

Direct communication with HR

Since the source of so much tension in a moveable marriage is the spouse's reliance on her partner to communicate with the company, you could consider asking for a regular correspondence (say, once a week for the first month, and thereafter once a month) to be set up between you and the HR person managing your husband's assignment.

When my husband was still working in our government's Department of Foreign Affairs and International Trade, the service started a newsletter with the not very creative but perfectly workable title *Direct Communication with Spouses*. The newsletter was definitely bureaucratic, but it was mailed (this was before e-mail was invented) directly to me, not to my husband. The articles covered job opportunities and other items of interest to me. In this electronic age, how difficult would it be for companies to e-mail spouses directly from headquarters or even set up the occasional conference call?

Spousal-company partnerships

Partnerships between spouses and the company can include all sorts of approaches, from spousal organizations or representatives who have some input into creating family policies to mentoring programs where each spouse is assigned another company spouse before and after relocation.

3M Corporation, based in Minneapolis, decided to use members of a spousal organization to set up the Foreign Services Employee Volunteer Program. Repatriation support has been one of this program's major successes. At a time when most companies do very little to welcome employees home from overseas assignments, 3M sets aside money and offers all-day training sessions. The idea for this program came from the spouses themselves.

DON'T FORGET THAT YOUR husband has needs, too, and that he may be finding it difficult to negotiate them with his company, never mind introducing your needs and those of your children. That's not to say that he shouldn't try! But take it from someone whose self-centeredness over the impact of our many moves could, at times, make the most selfish two-year-old look like a "sharer": it's important to understand what your partner is going through. You love him, after all. When I looked beyond the end of my nose and saw that my husband wasn't always having such an easy time of it, my marriage became stronger, the transitions easier to get through, and our family unit a much happier place to live in.

And remember, dinosaurs *did* eventually become extinct.

THREE

isolation and dependence

It was still the dark ages of technology when we made our first international relocation to Bangkok in the early 1980s. People were beginning to buy personal computers, known quaintly then as PCs, but most were using them only as glorified word processors or to store their favorite recipes. Fax machines were not yet popular home appliances, and neither satellite television dishes nor cellphones had become the ubiquitous symbols of high technology they are today.

Who could possibly have dreamed up a future that included e-mail? At the time, my idea of a higher power was a portable typewriter with a white-out ribbon built into it.

The Internet has been nothing short of a communications miracle in helping relocated families feel connected and less alone when they first arrive somewhere new. Isolation—and its common companion, desolation—are felt most keenly in the early days after moving to a new place, especially by a woman left alone to set up a home, put children into school, and build a new life.

Now, with wondrous ease (on a good technology day, anyway), e-mail provides instant communication with family and friends back home and helps relocated wives stay in touch with traveling husbands. For the relocating family, the Internet has opened the floodgates to an ever-increasing variety of useful websites, devoted to relocation information, support of every stripe, and online shopping. Likewise, improved telephone technology has made long-distance rates more affordable and has dramatically enhanced the quality of the calls themselves.

TROUBLESOME TELEPHONES COULD EASILY have become grounds for divorce when my husband and I first moved to Bangkok. Technically and metaphorically, we were always getting disconnected.

Phoning home to Canada, for instance, was practically a Victorian experience. Time-consuming protocols began with an overseas operator who was required to book the call. We would have to wait two hours or more for a call to go through. Precious conversations, limited to three minutes because of the exorbitant costs, consisted almost entirely of one party overlapping the other down an echo chamber of twelve time zones, each saying the same thing: "Can you hear me?"

Local calls were no easier. On really lonely days, I would try to "reach out and touch" my husband at work, just to hear a familiar voice. By the time the call got through to him, though, I was usually overwrought and hysterical. Trying to use local telephone lines that were so primitive it often took twenty minutes to get a dial tone would bring on a severe meltdown and only served to convince my husband that I had completely flipped out, an idea that had crossed my mind as well.

Because I very quickly became pregnant with our daughter after our move to Bangkok, I was definitely hormonally challenged, which is always good for a few buckets of tears over insignificant trifles like unworkable telephones—or what I was going to do with the rest of my life now that I had given up everything to get married and follow my husband's career. Pending motherhood gave me no immediate clues. I was too busy being cranky and miserable.

THE ADVENT OF HIGHER-TECHNOLOGY tools has changed how we manage the "externals" of a relocation in order to settle into new physical surroundings. But even the fanciest computer in the world, or a cellphone that can make calls from anywhere, including deep in a jungle, can't necessarily help you to process the "internals" of relocation: who you are, how you feel about yourself, and how you interact with your partner.

No one had advised me to think about these challenges, either culture shock in general or the shocks a marriage will experience after a physical transplant. Most couples never give their relationship a second thought, so consumed are they with the details of the relocation. Like so many women I know, I spent way too many hours alone in a strange new city fretting, belatedly, about my relationship and brooding about the loss of the person I used to be.

The biggest crime committed by my husband? From where I was—and that would usually be lying prone on a sofa, suffocated by the Thai heat—it was his good fortune to have an identity that both elevated and inspired him.

In the blink of a teary eye, my own self-image had

transformed from independent, confident, working broadcast journalist into hysterical, pregnant woman screaming into her phone in apartment 4D.

IN THE EARLY DAYS post-arrival, the toughest marital challenges can exist inside a woman's own head.

All that thinking deferred while you packed and organized a move is finally demanding its due. With no other adults around to talk to (your husband is probably working long hours to get up to speed in his new job), you talk to yourself. Those intense internal debates, argumentative but with no one fighting back, can make you feel like you are both acting and going mad. As a therapist once told me, the mind can be a dangerous place because there's no adult supervision in there.

"I always felt the biggest challenge for me were the quiet moments when my spouse was away, the kids were in bed, the house was clean and all the bills were paid. Sounds silly, doesn't it?" Jean, an American military spouse, married more than twenty years, wrote to me. "But that was the time when my mind could wander into places it shouldn't. It was the time I felt the responsibilities of my life the most. Slowing down and thinking of all the things I needed to do was more overwhelming than actually digging in and doing them."

When you have spent your day searching for breakfast cereal or a broom, and your husband comes home from work brimming with the confidence and stimulation of a new situation, frustration can spew out of you like emotional vomit. If that sounds gross, it's because women often *do* feel gross, as if some disgusting, malevolent creature has taken over their body and soul.

But this feeling is perfectly understandable once you figure out what's causing all that noise inside your head (not to mention prompting words you can't believe you are saying out loud) and making you feel less than warm and fuzzy towards your mate. Your initial isolation in a new place can lead to serious neediness and the attendant loss of independence. Right after a move, you rely on your partner to be everything from a friend to a sounding board to Mr. Fixit, helping you do stuff you've been trying to do by yourself all day. (Like hook up your computer, for instance.)

If you've always been an independent free spirit, this is a major marital aftershock of any move. Neediness is not attractive. It may also be a role reversal, depending on your marriage: he's suddenly the together one while you're the wounded, suffering bird. Without your independence as an emotional shield, you feel naked and vulnerable.

It becomes very tempting to bombard your partner with questions about *his* life because you need to have one yourself, even vicariously. Of course, it's usually the end of the working day when you do this, and he wants to sit back, relax, and not think about the office. You, on the other hand, are dying to hear every last detail.

But know this: *Your husband is not your girlfriend.*

In the absence of new women to hang out with, many relocated women start speaking to their husbands as if they were chatting with a girlfriend over coffee, seeking out minute details about new co-workers or neighbors that a man might not have noticed. We want and offer way too much information for their liking. And that's assuming they're even listening to us.

In a humorous but informative book called *Why Men Don't Listen and Women Can't Read Maps,* authors Barbara and Allan Pease make a biological and evolutionary case for the different ways in which men and women communicate. Among other things, say the authors, women "see" a situation differently. "What is commonly known as 'women's intuition' is mostly a woman's acute ability to notice small details and changes in the appearance or behavior of others. It's something that, throughout history, has bewildered men who play around—and are invariably caught."

A woman doesn't just *see* life in a way that is unlike a man's, she is also genetically hardwired to *listen* differently. As a result, write the authors, "A woman knows her children's friends, hopes, dreams, romances, secret fears, what they are thinking, how they are feeling, and usually, what mischief they are plotting. Men are vaguely aware of some short people also living in the house."

It's easy to let all that moving-related stuff swirling around in your head come spilling out when your partner just wants to read the paper and have a quiet drink. He is most definitely *not* in the mood to actively listen. Rather than encourage further conversation, our girlfriend patter can actually have the opposite effect, sending him fleeing to another room or causing him to eventually offer some profound, infuriating comment like "So, what's for dinner?"

My own husband's noncommunicativeness at the end of his working day used to heighten my feelings of neediness and insecurity about our relationship after a move. This is true for lots of other women, too. You feel disconnected from your partner, and although that may have been manageable in your old world, where you could step out the door and connect with someone else—a friend, a neighbor, even a shopkeeper—it can be scary in your new one.

After a while, I learned that my husband's silence most often came from exhaustion after coping with his new workplace all day. I had to learn not to take his need for quiet time personally. However, all this is just one more reason why you and your marriage partner need to engage in activities designed to enhance feelings of connection. Men usually have one surefire idea on this one (and will certainly listen if you make *that* suggestion), but I offer some other, nonphysical ways to communicate later in this chapter.

IT'S ONLY NATURAL TO feel invisible in a new place where you don't know anyone, no one knows you, and you are completely dependent upon one person—your mate—for everything. How could it be otherwise?

Please stop worrying that you've lost your mind along with your identity. Take heart in knowing that you're joining the ranks of thousands of other women who've been in similar straits and had *their* husbands tell them they were acting irrationally. Fine for the man to say, from the lofty heights of a person in possession of a business card and a job title. His identity hasn't disappeared into the moving ether where women and children are about as relevant as an employee's luggage: terribly necessary at first but, once unpacked, stored away until the next move.

In *Loving Him without Losing You: How to Stop Disappearing and Start Being Yourself,* therapist Beverly Engel sheds some light on the disappearing act many women do in relationships. She describes a disappearing woman as "a woman who tends to sacrifice her individuality, her beliefs, her career, her friends, and sometimes her sanity in a romantic relationship." Sound familiar?

Engel's book is aimed primarily at women who toss everyone and everything when involved with a man (you know, the kind of woman who breaks a date with another woman if a man calls to ask her out). However, it's interesting to note she felt her book would be of special interest to women "who are currently in a relationship in which they have submerged their needs or given over their power or individuality." No wonder I couldn't put the book down, especially when she presented a case study of a "disappearing" doctor's wife who could just as easily have been a woman who'd moved to support her husband's career.

This particular medical spouse had started out as the "strong one" in the relationship, actively engaged in community work and local politics and holding down a well-paying job. Her life changed when her husband graduated from medical school and became a doctor. (Go ahead, substitute the words "when her husband's job caused them to move.") Engel's interview subject offered a refrain I've heard countless times from mobile wives whose marriage has gone through that same shift in power: "Suddenly he was the important one and I was just the doctor's wife."

"People who had merely tolerated him because of our friendship suddenly started asking him for advice and began kowtowing to him," the medical spouse reported. "And I was expected to view him in a different light as well. He suddenly became more demanding of me, expecting me to run errands. I eventually bought into the belief that he was better than I was and of course, this made me feel more invisible."

The moral of the tale, according to therapist Engel, is that the problem of disappearing "goes beyond intellect, beyond self-esteem and self-confidence and involves the very core of a woman's identity. Even extremely attractive, wealthy, and famous women can become Disappearing Women when it comes to relationships."

No matter what their goals, most women who move for their husbands' jobs struggle to make themselves visible again in their new communities and to re-establish their identities and networks. Whether you are a long-time stay-at-home mom or a former CEO, you have to build some history in your new location, and it doesn't happen overnight. Identities and contacts can take years to re-establish when you are operating outside an office or a professional structure. Being "wife of" or "mother of" only takes your sense of self-worth so far.

But the longer it takes to reconnect with your surroundings, the more potential damage to your self-image you may be facing. So I highly recommend that, when women move, they get out there as quickly as possible and meet new people.

"Women's sense of self becomes very much organized around being able to maintain affiliation and relationships," American feminist psychiatrist Jean Baker Miller has noted in her fascinating research into women at the Stone Center for Developmental Service and Studies at Wellesley University. "Eventually, for many women, the threat of disruption of connection is perceived not as loss of a relationship but as something closer to a total loss of self."

Dr. Miller's theories about relationships have at their core a belief that growth-fostering relationships are central to a person's well-being. The absence of relationships and connections, she believes, can lead to psychological problems. Mobile spouses in particular are not part of her research, but her theories apply well to our population.

Think about it: if a woman survives and thrives on relationships and connection, and a relocation forces her to abandon those altogether, how does that make her feel? And how does it affect the one major relationship that remains constant, that with her husband? If a woman feels insecure, or not quite her confident self at the beginning of a relocation, is it any wonder she often feels like she's losing her mind as well?

The situation can be particularly depressing for a woman who feels she's become invisible in the *only* adult relationship she may have for weeks or months after a relocation. Some women feel like the hired (non-paid) help, trapped with the moving representatives or other service people while their husbands are off having a life. A wife can quickly become irritated with a partner who doesn't seem to notice she's not as overjoyed about the move as he is or who chooses to ignore her feelings out of self-interest. He's having a great time in his new job and doesn't want her throwing cold water all over it. She, however, may be marking time until they can move home again.

Many women feel conflicted: they are having a hard time in their new location, but they love and understand their husbands nonetheless. Sally, a thirty-something wife and mother who responded to my survey, wrote: "I felt I lost my identity. I gave up my career, and I resent that. But

I love my husband and have to tell myself that is what's most important." Don't we all have similar sentiments? Have I mentioned that I love my own husband very much, too? (Remember, he will be reading this book!)

It's not unusual for a woman to look to her husband for affirmation of her identity, especially when he's often the only person within a thousand-mile radius who knows who she used to be. It won't be nearly as easy to find that affirmation as it will be to find a new girl-friend for a coffee date. Yet even so, after a move, her husband becomes the center of a woman's adult universe by default, and because women are conditioned to seek male approval, she struggles for his attention. When she doesn't get it, because her husband's busy, away a lot, or not smart enough to figure out what she's craving, both her identity is compromised and her feelings are hurt. Worse, things may be said that can't be taken back.

For many women, it's not only being ignored that bothers them—they also want to receive proper recognition and acknowledgment for the part they're playing in the relocation. "Gaining my husband's respect was critical for me," Yvonne McNulty, a recently married Australian woman in her thirties, told me about her first relocation. "I know he has always respected me, but it's important to me that he also respects my contribution to our life, our marriage, and our home."

After feeling lousy for the first year after she moved and constantly questioning if the move had been worth it, Yvonne decided to go back to school to complete studies that had been interrupted earlier in her life. She told me her self-esteem went "sky-high" when her partner began respecting the research she was doing into the corporate management of relocation, inspired by her own experience. "But most of all," she said, "my husband respects how I turned my situation around."

Gloria Steinem, author of the seminal 1992 work *Revolution from Within: A Book of Self-Esteem,* would have been pleased at how Yvonne took charge of her life. "The art of life is not controlling what happens to us," wrote Steinem, "but *using* what happens to us."

Women who equate identity with purpose will feel lost in their new setting until they find work, a play group for their young children, a local university where they can sign up for courses, or other useful and productive ways to spend their days.

Each time my own family moved, even back home to Canada, I would go through the same isolating and demoralizing experience, with only minor variations, of re-establishing my identity and finding purpose by setting new personal and professional goals. Like clockwork, when my own internal balance was shaky, my marriage struggled to regain its equilibrium. Over and over, my marriage got back on track only once I'd figured out how to spend my days and made some—any—outside connection to my new community.

In other words, once I was more or less happy again, everything was all right again in the marriage. "Don't be mad and don't be sad," my older sister once said to me about marriage. I've always wanted to cross-stitch those words or paint them ten feet high.

The repetitious post-arrival syndrome can feel like being trapped in *Groundhog Day,* the riotous American comedy in which actor Bill Murray's character could never break free of the same day and the same feelings. Settling into a new place, with no one to speak to, an absent husband, and an apartment or house to organize, can be a terrible, lonely rut a woman finds herself in over and over again, even after knowing what to expect.

Like many others, though, I learned that the feelings of isolation eventually lift. This knowledge is a life raft that experienced relocating spouses learn to cling to for comfort. As Joan, a woman whose husband's job took her through five relocations, told me: "I may be lonely and feel a bit useless today, but when I start working again next week at a volunteer job, and make some new friends, I know things will pick up again."

THERE IS AN INTENSE loneliness to work through in the early days and weeks after a move, and these feelings are bound to manifest themselves in the dynamics of the relationship and in everyday life.

Writing to me from a posting abroad, Barbara, a fifty-something American diplomatic spouse who's been through multiple moves, put it this way when I asked for a description of her feelings upon arrival.

Sad: because I left children in boarding school.
Worried: because our finances are worse than glum.
Happy: because for once, we're in a nice place and
maybe family will finally visit.
Useless: because I feel incompetent, lazy, negative, crabby,
incommunicative, unreasonable and insane.
But the worst and strongest feeling with all moves is lonely.

She's certainly not alone in having those feelings.

Therapist Phyllis Adler says that, in her London practice with expatriate spouses, the two biggest challenges her female clients face are coping with children (which I address in chapter 6) and making friends. These days, life is not as conducive as it once was to walking outside, knocking on the door of a new neighbor, and finding a welcoming hello to greet you. In today's busy world, spontaneity has been lost, and people are often too "busy being busy" to take time out for a new person. Which only makes a woman feel worse, of course, and more alone.

From day one of my marriage, the working model for my loneliness took shape as it does for so many women: in response to my partner's incessant business travel. If I were to add up the length of time my husband has been on the road from wherever we happened to be living, I'd likely discover we've only really been "together" about half as long as I thought. (On a positive note, I have divorced friends who feel they'd still be married if their partners had traveled as much as mine!)

I have often called myself a "single parent without dating privileges" as a way of making light of my loneliness when my road-warrior partner is away. Jean, the American military wife I quoted earlier in the chapter, told me she also feels like a single parent. "But who wants dating privileges?" she asked me facetiously. "When my husband is gone, I don't have to worry about putting down the toilet seat. I don't have to fix my hair or put on a happy face to make someone else feel good, either. The best part of his being gone, though, is his coming home. There aren't many women who have had as many honeymoons as I have, and that's special."

Not all reunions after a business trip resemble a honeymoon, though. Although I may feel lonely when my husband is away, that doesn't mean I always find it easy to reconnect with him once he's home again. Inevitably, something (usually involving floods, as we seem to have bad water karma) has gone wrong while he's been gone, so I typically have some irritation to work out before I'm willing to feel friendly again. To deal with this, we instituted the twenty-four-hour holding rule: no expectations of the other for at least the first full day, which gives us both the time and space to get used to each other again.

My own experience with managing expectations leads conveniently to another key feature of the post-arrival time—the anger and resentment many women experience almost immediately after a move.

SINCE MY MARRIAGE WAS barely a year old when we moved to Bangkok, I fretted constantly about the state of it. What would I possibly have to say to my husband when he came home from the embassy that didn't sound boring or, worse, carry an extremely high risk of being out-and-out confrontational? Feeling the size of an elephant and looking like one, along with a bad case of pregnancy acne, made me worry so much I would cry incessantly to him about it. (Those hormones at work again.) A crying elephant with a rash of pimples across her forehead (and across my expanding belly, too) isn't sexy at the best of times, and especially not after my husband had worked all day with some extraordinarily beautiful women.

On the days my husband wasn't off at yet another

fancy welcoming luncheon and I actually could reach him on the phone, the edge in my voice hinted at the intense jealousy and resentment boiling inside. I couldn't stand the fact that my partner could sit all day in an office with secretaries to place his calls (in Thai when required, of course). Drivers took him to his appointments while I had to struggle with the local conveyances, usually with only three wheels, to locations such as the office of the doctor who would deliver our first child. My husband was surrounded by people he could talk to all day long while I sat alone in a rocking chair on the balcony of our apartment, watching mangy dogs eat our garbage.

I could have spit nails.

A hilarious but enlightening article on resentment that appeared in *O Magazine* in 2002 informed me that I would have been better off throwing a rusty fork at my partner's forehead. That's what writer Allison Glock confessed wanting to do to her husband when the laundry or some other household task remained undone.

Glock's article contained some informed research on resentment, which her sources (among them her mother, who is a couples therapist) defined as "what happens when anger builds up and can't find expression or resolution. It's when you personalize behavior you shouldn't." Glock could blow up about the laundry, but it was "really about how, if he loved me, he would intuit the need to do the laundry."

Many of us want our husbands to know how upset we are about a move without actually having to tell them. "I don't know of a single husband who has taken a course in ESP," a wise-beyond-her-years twenty-four-year-old mobile wife named Andrea wrote to me. "If you don't tell him how you are feeling—overwhelmed, anxious, scared—how can he know?"

Anger and resentment, like low self-esteem, are important ongoing challenges of moveable marriages, and they underscore all the other challenges, from money to intimacy to raising mobile children. The sooner couples negotiate or mediate their way out of the scenarios that breed those feelings, the better off the marriage will be.

It isn't just a new city or a new country that can throw your relationship into shock after a move. It's that intangible concept of change itself: changes in your everyday environment and changes in your partner.

"My husband underwent a personality change after we moved," Susan, an American diplomatic wife, wrote to me. It remains one of my favorite lines, because I have heard it in so many forms from others. A moveable marriage brings about personal change in both of the marriage partners as well as in how they get along.

Any marriage that undergoes a change (think of the addition of a baby or when an in-law has to move in) will experience some sort of fallout. Whether it's the change in physical environment, the change in work (only one person may have a paid job), or the changes many women perceive in their husbands after a move, there will be a period of time when all of these things are swirling around in your head, making you feel totally disoriented.

Noted "change guru" William Bridges writes in *Transitions: Making Sense of Life's Changes* that families are "systems" not unlike an organization, and members "are not autonomous entities that happen to be together, but are actually parts of a larger whole and are affected by anything that happens to that whole." Moving definitely qualifies as a major *happening*.

"Any time any member of a system changes," writes Bridges, "the other members will feel a twinge . . . and of course, partners in any intimate relationship react with alarm to unexpected changes in the other person."

Panic is a natural result of a change in one's spouse. "My spouse thrives on change," wrote Susan, the American diplomatic wife. "I shrink and shrivel. Shrunken and shriveled persons don't make good partners."

The good news, says William Bridges, is that relationships forced into change can in fact grow if the transition is handled properly. "Each has the opportunity to be more whole, more complete as a person. The relationship can then be renegotiated. This process of renegotiation must take place many times during a long-term relationship if it is to stay vital and provide both partners with a setting for their continued development. When a couple can share this awareness [of change] and explore its significance in their present situation, they can transform a threatening difficulty into an opportunity."

I FELT LIKE A FAILURE as a mobile wife more times than I can remember. Could I, would I, *ever* be happy? That's what my husband asked me many times in the early days of our moveable marriage, until I got wise to the emotional rhythms of our peripatetic lifestyle. After that, I asked him for time to "sort myself out" after each move (six months sounded about right) before he threw that question at me. As a person who had always felt I could handle change, I couldn't understand why I wasn't coping. What was wrong with me, anyway?

Obviously I've learned a thing or two along the way, including the fact that there was nothing wrong with me and that my feelings were natural. But most important of all, I've learned this: at the end of the day, it is up to *me* to dig myself out of the hole. Yes, a company may make matters worse, and yes, men can be less than understanding, but women must take personal responsibility for their own welfare and not shift the blame (at least, not all of it) onto others.

"We are a species not so easily made happy," writes author Anne Roiphe in *Married: A Fine Predicament.* She wasn't writing about the moveable members of our species, but she certainly could have been. When my husband would ask me what precisely would make me happy, I couldn't admit that it would please me enormously if he were a little less happy himself.

If you are feeling isolated in your new location, here are some tried-and-true strategies for digging yourself out.

Learn to communicate

My husband and I had no game plan for coping with the changes that every one of our relocations brought to our relationship. The issues differed with every move we made, whether domestic or international, because each time we were at a new age and stage of life. I've since learned just how key communication is to the successful moveable marriage.

When partners can begin to see—and understand— what's going on for the other person, this empathy is a lifesaver for the relationship and a good chance to strengthen the marriage. I've heard from many women who believe their marriages grew stronger because, after a move, they and their husbands were forced to work as a team and rely on each other.

"I think strong marriages won't suffer, weak marriages won't last, and 'normal' marriages can go in either direction," wrote Jane, a thirty-eight-year-old mother of two boys who has relocated three times. "Marriages that do stand get very strong, in my opinion."

Of course, *both* parties have to be listening.

Acknowledge that women and men listen differently

Employee Assistance Program specialist Sally Lipscomb believes that high on the list of skills couples should develop is *supportive listening*. In her view, that's listening without criticizing or letting your own feelings intrude. Couples can debrief at the end of the day using fixed ground rules: no criticism or skepticism, just true listening without personal emotion attached.

If my husband and I had acquired that skill before our first major move, he might have kept his mouth shut instead of admitting, when I complained about how awful I looked during pregnancy, "Frankly, Robin, I have to be honest and say I just don't find you attractive right now." He had to fetch many buckets to capture my tears after that gaffe.

"The only way a woman gets problems out of her mind is by talking about them to acknowledge them," write Barbara and Allan Pease in *Why Men Don't Listen*. "When a woman talks at the end of the day, her objective is to discharge the problems, not to find conclusions or solutions." But a man, say the authors, will see continual chatter as a plea for solutions. With his analytical brain, he will continually interrupt the woman to offer suggestions.

Ironically, men are constantly telling women to stop interrupting them. That's because a man's sentences are solution oriented, according to the Peases. "A man needs to get to the end of the sentence, otherwise the conversation seems pointless . . . He can't multi-track various points at different times in the conversation . . . and this is a foreign concept to a woman. She multi-tracks to build rapport and make him feel important."

To add insult to injury, the authors note that "in a typical male/female conversation, 76 per cent of interruptions are made by men!" (That's their exclamation point, by the way, not mine.)

To get a man to listen, try this: give him advance notice that you want to talk, provide an agenda, set a time limit, and tell him whether or not you are looking for solutions to specific things such as parenting issues or housekeeping matters. "Most men will agree to a request like that because it has a time, a place, and an objective—all the things that appeal to the male brain. And he's not expected to do any work," advise the authors of *Why Men Don't Listen*.

And remember what I said earlier: he's not your girlfriend, so self-edit what you are discharging in all that chatter.

Join everything
If connections, relationships, and finding a purpose are key to our well-being and identity, then once the moving boxes are emptied and the stress lines on your face have

more or less relaxed, it's time to start joining. Sign up for everything that looks remotely interesting.

A newcomers' club (something I avoided until I learned how foolish a decision that was) is exactly right for you. You *are* a newcomer, remember? Put aside any previous disdain for women's groups. They can be a lifeline, and their member directories are your best phone book in a new community. So what if you don't want to learn flower arranging or cooking without fat? Women's groups offer a lot more than hands-on classes these days. Or join an exercise class.

If your move is international, sign up for language classes as soon as possible. I met one of my best friends to this day in a Thai language class in Bangkok. Volunteer in the community or on a committee at your children's school. If nothing else, these activities will get you outside both your door and your own head.

Avoid the temptation to drink alone

Your husband's long working days, or suppers that often go cold as you wait for him, can create a potentially dangerous, habit-forming scenario. There's a temptation to open a bottle of wine while you wait, and if the wait is a long one, before you know it the bottle is empty. When this happens on a regular basis, it's no longer just a "nice glass of wine to keep you company." Similarly, taking any one of the exploding number of anti-anxiety or anti-depressant drugs on the market "just to get through the early days" can sometimes lead to a serious dependency.

One day, when my children and I were trapped in a Beijing hotel room awaiting the return of their father, I opened a bottle of duty-free Scotch, thinking that a small drink would relieve my anger and anxiety. By the time my husband showed up, I had indulged in more than one shot. I must have been very uninhibited about my resentment in front of my children, since my daughter (who was only seven at the time) claims she can still recall the advice I gave her: "Grow up and be a man if you want to get the best deal!"

Increased consumption of alcohol and a reliance on prescribed medications can both be fallout effects of loneliness and isolation. Please seek professional help if you find that your use of either alcohol or pills is getting out of hand.

What about work?

Work may be a top priority in your new location, not only to give your life purpose but for reasons of cold hard cash. After a move, it's challenging to network into a new work world, and too often women jump into a bad job in order to feel settled and then have to figure out (with the help of a noncommunicative husband) how to get out of it. I talk more about this in the next chapter. But if *only* work will give you back your identity, then you need to go for it.

I NOW LOOK BACK NOSTALGICALLY on the challenging early days of moving our marriage to Asia. Our experiences there make up many humorous chapters of our marriage folklore. But at the time, the privileged life I was leading, with a beautiful apartment, a wonderful Thai maid to do everything for me, exotic surroundings, and a great cuisine that I didn't have to slave over to enjoy, completely escaped me. My loneliness and isolation had taken firm control of my common sense and gratitude.

Such self-absorption can be distressing, but William Bridges' words are comforting: "Distress is not a sign that anything has gone wrong, but that something is changing." Furthermore, he believes it's only by understanding the importance of the transition process, anticipating times of anxiety, and expecting that one or the other partner in the marriage will be threatened by the changes that the ground will be cleared for new growth.

Writing about the isolation, the identity crisis, and the loneliness that a woman often experiences after a move would be depressing if I wasn't constantly reminding myself—as I want to remind you—that identifying challenges doesn't mean they are necessarily going to arise. Or that, if they do, they will be our undoing. However, as the Boy Scouts say, it's always better to be prepared.

FOUR

dual career challenges

For over twenty years, I've seized every opportunity to kick up a public fuss about dual career challenges, mobility, and marriage. My head's been banging against walls so hard I have bruises to show for it. I've stuck my neck out when I should have kept my head low and my big mouth shut. It certainly didn't help my husband, in his first career as a diplomat, to be married to a none-too-diplomatic wife.

I've ranted about it all: the professional disruptions and difficulties for the accompanying spouse; the identity crisis and loss of self-confidence when women's careers are abandoned or put on hold; the power shifts in formerly equal marriages that favor the primary earner.

My loudest protests have called for more organizational support for a spouse's career during a company-sponsored move. Given that "spousal reluctance to give up career" can be the biggest deal-breaker in the relocation of a valuable employee, and that the dual career challenge is seen by so many women as the biggest relocation challenge, there's method in my madness.

My credentials for making trouble are impeccable. I have experienced all the highs and lows of a self-invented career path in which I chose to put my family's needs first instead of single-mindedly chasing brass rings.

My first and foremost identity is as a full-time mom. But while I proudly feel my well-adjusted, happy children are my greatest *personal* success, I have persistently felt like a *professional* failure. Why? Because I barely earn enough money to buy a cup of coffee. Yes, I know my feelings of failure ignore all the unpaid labor I have done for over two decades, and if I ever totaled *that* up, I would join the ranks of millionaires. But that doesn't matter to me, or any of the thousands of women like me, when we're having a bad day.

I've always pointed the finger of blame at my partner and his career, although I've had few kind words for his former employer, the Government of Canada. Nor do society's ways of validating people with a dollar sign thrill me much.

Given my track record of advocacy and rabble-rousing, however, I'm surprising even myself with what I want to say next: I may have been wrong about how relocation impacts on a career.

I HAVEN'T BEEN WRONG about the many unique career challenges for a relocating spouse. These can and do get in the way of an otherwise healthy relationship if you let them. But it seems I may have been mistaken in predicting where my career would sit two decades after my departure from a structured working life in my chosen profession.

As I watch and read about women of my own generation who stayed in the workforce to try to set the world on fire, only to find decades down the road that they can't wait to get out, it may be—gasp!—that mobility deserves more of a rave than a rant.

For all my moaning, moving turned out to be the best thing that ever happened to my career. It certainly has made my life a lot more interesting. The lack of a structured career path (in countries such as China, it would have been laughable for a diplomat's wife to try to obtain press credentials) forced me to think outside my comfort zone. I had to be creative in figuring out how to adapt my skills and interests, take more risks, and rely entirely on my own devices.

I've been forced to network a lot, and as a result I've created long-lasting friendships with women around the world who continue to be enormously supportive of my work. And I work as a team with my husband. How many men would help their wives create a website using only HTML *for Dummies?* Only true love could have survived the technological nervous breakdowns we had over bringing my website into cyberspace.

With the scenery always shifting and no one to turn to for advice, I had to hunt a lot harder for my passion. And when the hunt is more difficult, what you're looking for is a whole lot sweeter when you find it.

THIS CAREER EPIPHANY DIDN'T come to me quickly, given the mantra of my baby boom generation: *You can have it all!* No, you can't, Gloria Steinem told us, and she was right, in retrospect.

I rarely reread my own books. Perhaps if I did, I'd have stumbled earlier across the definitions of the word "career" set out in my first book, *A Wife's Guide.* It was there I first proclaimed "career" to be a man's word, driven by male values and driving women crazy as they tried to live up to its notions of success.

When career is viewed instead as "a path through life," it allows women to incorporate all that is important to them, whether it's raising children, volunteering in their communities, looking after home and family, or pursuing a vocation.

However, it would seem I've been advocating that women take a long-term view of relocated careers, yet always managed to be destroyed personally by short-term setbacks. So much for being an expert.

My *aha!* moment happened almost casually at my local library one day as I sat submerged in paper and books, trying to process the ton of opinions that have been offered on the subject of dual careers. Procrastinating hopelessly over the materials paralyzed my writing routine. A deafening, distracting confusion was going on inside my head.

After a while, I realized that, along with my writing, I was conveniently avoiding serious introspection about my *own* dual career marriage, and how my work and values system have been woven into it. Some soul-searching was required, so I pushed aside the reports, grabbed a blank piece of paper, and began writing down some hard questions for myself, the kind that could only be asked and answered from the lofty position of middle age, menopause, and a marriage that had made it through ten domestic and international moves *and* a twenty-year anniversary.

Did my career go down the toilet because I married a mobile guy? Could I blame him and the government for everything? Could I honestly say that there was something else I'd rather be doing at this point in my life? Did I want to be viewed or even judged solely by what I do rather than who I am? No, no, no, and definitely no.

And, finally, would I really like to have a "big job" and report to an office every morning, be stuck there all day, do stuff I don't want to do or work I might not believe in, or, worst of all, wear big-girl clothing every weekday, including panty hose and uncomfortable shoes? *No way.*

Identifying all the positives that have emerged from what felt too often like a dark, negative hole of professional oblivion, I was struck that things have turned out so well.

Go and get yourself a piece of paper right now and start making a list of the positive repercussions of moving on your work. You might be, as the Brits would say, gobsmacked by your answers. I was in a state of shock for a few days myself before returning to my computer.

I'm not alone in feeling that a new world opened up for me once I left everything behind and jumped off the proverbial career cliff. I've heard many inspirational stories similar to my own.

I CORRESPONDED WITH RUTH after her fourteenth move, the first international one her family had made. Ruth has managed an active career as an interior designer for more than twenty years, and she is convinced that constant relocations were a bonus.

"My creativeness extends far beyond the drafting board, especially when it comes to a clientele," she wrote. "I've definitely had to think outside the 'box' and also redefine my role to accommodate my husband's frequent moves and, more importantly, my children's needs through the years."

When her children were little, Ruth opted for computer-aided design because she could do that at home. In another town, she saw a tremendous need for a drapery workroom, so she acquired a few new skills and designed and fabricated window treatments while her son played "fort" under her sewing table. In all, Ruth has run seven different small businesses from home.

Now that she's living abroad, she's not allowed to work without a permit—a permit that is very difficult to obtain. But this hasn't stopped her from learning. Surrounded by fascinating design history and craftsmanship in the country she'll call home for several years, she's taking full advantage of her time to study its design culture.

"My career has in no way ended," Ruth wrote. "I'm merely in an enrichment and redefinition period, which wouldn't be possible without my incredibly supportive husband and extremely flexible children."

Or take the story of Arlene, an American living in the United Kingdom who has professionalized her volunteerism. Arlene has held fifteen leadership positions on boards or as committee chair as she's moved around the world with her engineer husband. She sees every relocation—she and her husband have moved from home base in the United States to Asia and then to Europe, where they presently live—as offering new opportunities to either hone existing skills and talents or learn new ones.

"Volunteering has had a positive effect on my marriage," she wrote to me. "It provides me with ongoing opportunities for personal growth and fulfillment. Although I do depend on my husband's paycheck, I find

I am not dependent upon him nor his career for my own personal satisfaction or self-esteem."

For other women, the family is their vocation. And as any mother can confirm, that can be a full-time job.

"My career moves with my husband," a military wife named Lynn wrote to me, "because I am a stay-at-home mom." That line is brilliant in the self-awareness it illustrates. As a stay-at-home mom, you can and do set up shop anywhere.

"Raising children may be the most important job in the world, but you can't put it on a résumé," writes former economics reporter Ann Crittenden in *The Price of Motherhood: Why the Most Important Job in the World Is Still the Least Valued.* Or can you? Like a company broken up so that subsidiaries can be sold separately, the thousand-and-one skills acquired in managing a household can also be broken down and finessed on your cv.

Either way, these stories serve to demonstrate that no matter what your skill set, goals, or profession, success never comes without self-knowledge, hard work, and, sometimes, considerable heartache along the way.

Here's one of my own stories. After all those relocations and more than twenty years as a journalist, I moved to Vancouver, my present location, and found myself writing articles about the funeral industry. *American Cemetery*, a magazine I'm sure serves an indispensable purpose for undertakers, was not my ideal writing market. It wasn't, say, *The New York Times Magazine.* But it was the publication I wrote for, and not incidentally, I worked with some great people once I got over feeling, pun intended, dead and buried professionally.

Mobility has given a great number of women a positive,

optimistic conviction that one door closing always means another one will be opening. That just may not be obvious in the short term. And there can be other priceless rewards, such as the ability to measure the success of your life's work in intangibles that have nothing to do with money, once you've adjusted your attitude and got your sense of humor firmly in place.

"I was so determined to have a work identity, it actually got in the way of what I really wanted to do," says an interview subject in Elizabeth Perle McKenna's enlightening book *When Work Doesn't Work Anymore: Women, Work and Identity.* "It was more important for me to prove I could be successful in the short term than to pursue a long-term dream."

TAKING A LONG-TERM VIEW of anything these days is difficult. We've become short-term thinkers, living in an instant society built on speed. Most of us are too busy to think beyond answering today's batch of e-mail. To think long-term about something as important as our professional lives requires a suspension of our faith in that high-tech global village. Every day, there are more incursions into our personal space. Who has the time, inclination, or stillness to think about important matters when confronted with limitless choices about everything? Easier to just point, click, and send.

Australian Yvonne McNulty has been giving a lot of thought to the subject of career choices (her own and other mobile women's) in her academic research about spouses and human resource management. She believes that spouses need more corporate support for their intrinsic needs, which include coming to terms with the identity challenges posed by a loss of career. Too much attention, she says, is focused on the more tangible (and easier to address) challenges such as money, housing, or schools.

Yvonne is not yet raising children, and she came of age intellectually and professionally in the bright, optimistic light of feminism's utopia, where career choices and parenthood could supposedly go hand in hand.

Her generation has learned, however, that choice can often be more illusion than reality, and she is the wiser for knowing that. What took me over twenty years to figure out seems to have taken Yvonne only eighteen months into her relocation to the United States with her British husband. "If I hadn't moved, I suspect I would have gone on for years in a career I didn't particularly like simply because it was the 'right thing to do' rather than go find something I am passionate about," she wrote.

SINCE THIS IS A BOOK about moveable marriages, it's important for me to point out that you won't find direct career advice here. (Although some is bound to sneak in—I just can't help myself sometimes.) There are lots of good books and websites to assist you with career matters during relocation, and you can find many of them listed in the back of this book.

However, I believe it's even more critical to know about healthy ways of discussing your professional challenges with your husband, so that you can receive the support you need from him. Sometimes he won't get it, of course. And let me reassure you that those tense, hurtful conversations about career pop up all over the place, not only in *your* home. When I was discussing the content of this chapter with my husband as we relaxed in our garden one beautiful afternoon, a fight almost broke out. And I was agreeing with him!

It would be simple to spout all the thousands of statistics and studies that tackle this wide subject of dual careers, but that's not my goal either. I don't want to obfuscate an emotional issue with statistics.

"Take the emotion out of your business," my husband would advise me when I stayed up all night crying about a business partnership that had gone wrong.

"Are you out of your mind?" I demanded. "Women are all *about* emotion!"

The pressures of maintaining or chasing after two careers in a relocated marriage are as much emotional as practical. That's why they can make us feel overwhelmed and stressed out about our relationships. If it were just a job we were after, things would be different, but the stakes here are infinitely higher than a nine-to-five place to park ourselves. It's about who we think we *are,* and about coming to understand our new role in a moveable marriage.

"Dual career marriages have two husbands and no wife." I found that terrific turn of phrase in several sources, among them *More Equal Than Others: Women and Men in Dual Career Marriages,* by Rosanna Hertz. She writes that "all marriages are shaped by work," since work determines a family's lifestyle, standard of living, and social status.

Hertz believes the dual career marriage "challenges a number of principles of the traditional marriage. Work and its rewards still shape a couple's life chances; but instead of a single career or job defining marital roles, there are two careers, qualifying each spouse as a bread-winner." Hence, the two husbands.

During a relocation, an accompanying spouse, who may up until that point have been one of those husbands and breadwinners, suddenly reverts to being the wife, and perhaps the only parent, too. The traditional family roles (husband at work, wife at home) emerge as if by sheer force of nature. This new role propels the woman out the door, not to a job of her own but, none too happily, to run the errands and drop off her husband at the office.

This change in role *description,* not role *playing,* usually begins a chain of unpleasant events. It's not that women aren't already used to assuming multiple roles in their lives, including the running of a household. But relocation knocks out the role that may be most important to a woman because it defines her more than any of the others.

"One of the biggest needs I have is to be recognized for my own achievements," wrote Carol, a mother of two in her forties who had moved twice to follow her husband. "I don't consider housework anything to be proud of. I have a good brain and love challenges and stimulation and the satisfaction of overcoming these challenges. There has been a profound absence of these important factors since I moved. My husband has seen the scope of my frustration and unhappiness, and I believe he would happily give up the convenience of having me around to cook and clean in order that I could feel fulfilled as well."

Most women expressed a similar view about their

husbands. Indeed, my own partner claims that each time we moved he prayed to an unseen career god to grant me something to do that would make me happy (and earn money, too, if there really was such a god).

University of Oklahoma professor Michael Harvey, writing in *Human Resource Planning* about dual career challenges, makes a distinction between dual career and dual earning couples. "Dual career couples are frequently defined as both partners employed and psychologically committed to their work . . . or employed in upwardly mobile jobs; whereas, the dual income and/or earner couple has both the husband and wife who earn an income outside the household."

The relevant words here are "psychologically committed." Many of us are driven to pursue our passion by neurotic obsession rather than in a quest for the glories of fame and fortune. That can often make it more stressful to communicate with a partner about an abandoned career. An ever-pragmatic man might say to a wife committed to her work in volunteerism, for instance, "Why are you so upset about giving up something that doesn't make any money?"

WHEN ONE PARTNER TECHNICALLY doesn't "do" anything outside the home after a relocation, but did something outside the home before the move, there's bound to be a crisis. We define ourselves by our work, and our work nourishes our self-esteem and self-confidence. Since a woman thrives on relationships and connections (many of which come via the workplace) and on the work that identified her place in the world, when those have been lost, even temporarily, she can feel invisible.

She will also be spoiling for a good fight, especially if she and her husband have just returned from a social gathering where she's been asked what she does, only to have her tongue-tied answer elicit a blank stare and a social cut.

Ann Crittenden wrote *The Price of Motherhood* to examine not only the considerable economic benefits lost by women when they take on raising children, but also the loss of identity when they become mothers and their families reconfigure into traditional roles. Reading her book, I could have replaced "motherhood" with "relocation" dozens of times. The price of relocation to follow a husband's career is eerily similar to the costs incurred by jumping onto the so-called Mommy Track. The identity crisis is almost exactly the same.

"I was at a Washington, D.C., cocktail party, when someone asked, 'What do you do?' I replied that I was a new mother, and they promptly vanished," writes Crittenden. "I was the same person this stranger might have found worthwhile had I said I was a foreign correspondent for *Newsweek*, a financial reporter for the *New York Times* or a Pulitzer prize nominee, all of which had been true. But as a mother, I had shed status like the skin off a snake."

Crittenden bumped through what writer Elizabeth Perle McKenna describes in *When Work Doesn't Work Anymore* as "the rocky transition from a work-based identity to one based on what was important . . . The issue here is the conflict itself, the tear between a life built around who we thought we should be as career women and who we have become in the process of our lives."

For our purposes, that life is a moveable one, and the

"tear" is too often with our mate. You're freaking out about who you were and apparently are no longer, and he's not getting it one little bit. He thinks *he* knows who you are: you're his wife and the mother of his children. He also knows who you used to be, but he's not shouting that from any rooftops. Research suggests that when asked what his wife used to do, a relocated employee will often downplay her former job. Why? He feels guilty for yanking her away from it.

WHOEVER THINKS OF GRIEF in connection with a career? The question should really be: Why haven't we thought about it more? We've always associated grief with the loss of a loved one, not with the loss of something intangible like a career or an identity. But make no mistake. Grief is all about loss, and who can deny how much is lost when a career is abandoned?

During a relocation, a healthy woman will experience the different stages of grief (beginning with denial) and work her way to the end of the grief spectrum. Unfortunately, many of us get stuck in the anger phase, clinging to it for dear life. Anger can be a convenient distraction from thinking about tough topics that may hit too close to home.

"Before a woman can even accept a relocation as the accompanying spouse, she needs to do some anticipatory grieving," says Canadian grief counselor and marriage therapist Elva Mertick, who also works with relocating couples in Calgary and abroad. "She must acknowledge she will be giving up a part of herself (that is, her career), which she has created as part of her self-image."

No one can move forward with life after someone

close to them dies until all the stages of grief are explored. Neither can a relocated woman get on with her life without working through these stages after a move.

"One of the things I've learned is that I was not actually mourning the loss of a career but grieving over the loss of the choice to have one," Aussie Yvonne told me. "This is a big distinction that didn't twig with me for the first eighteen months."

Once she acknowledged her grief, Yvonne says she woke up a totally different woman. "Everything I did from that day forward I did with a different attitude. So maybe I didn't have the choice to pursue a traditional career (job interviews, consistent salary, corporate environment, putting on a suit every day, everything I was used to), but I had something better: the choice to invent a new one."

Having the first choice taken away from her made Yvonne rethink "the whole career thing." Nowadays, she's passionate about changing the way companies manage relocation for accompanying spouses. She credits her early awareness to her research, which included hundreds of surveys she administered through her website, *www.thetrailingspouse.com.*

"Just reading all of these women moan and complain has been like living the experience several hundred times over. Knowing I wasn't the first woman to go through it, and definitely won't be the last, was unbelievably comforting, and I think it took away the 'beat myself up' mentality that I automatically imposed upon my 'pathetic life.' I felt normal when I found out that this, too, shall pass."

Yvonne found a creative way to deal with her own

grief, and grief counselor Mertick agrees that focusing on creativity during the grieving period is a very healthy alternative. "One woman I was seeing who had moved to Africa tended to call her mother almost every day during the low time. This was useful for support but not useful in being able to move on. Then she got connected with a group of women who were exploring their creativity and trying to use the other side of their brains."

When Mertick saw her client later, the woman was having the first show of her artwork, had discovered new talents and skills, and had totally changed her image of herself. "So my advice is that, while women can hold onto previous colleagues to keep in the loop of a former profession, it's equally important for a woman to explore other parts of herself and her potential. It can be a great time for discovery."

AND THEN THERE'S MONEY. There's *always* the money issue. In relocation, there's never enough of it. Even if an organization pays for the move, it's amazing how easy it is to spend money moving into a new house or apartment, signing up for new services, and so on. From my privileged middle-class vantage point, I could blithely say that money doesn't matter, but I'd be lying. In the first place, when *hasn't* money mattered? In the second, I'd be ignoring the fact that money, like work, determines a couple's lifestyle.

I write more on the subject of money in the next chapter, but for now, suffice to say that when one career is tossed, there are bound to be power struggles over how a couple spends money and who has the final say in how it gets spent. The short answer? The major earner.

As you're sorting out your feelings about work after a relocation, there's something else you need to face boldly. Honest answers to the following questions can help you find your way out of the moving maze you may find yourself in. Did your move cause a career crisis that's led to problems in your marriage? Or would those issues have arisen regardless?

Career crises for women are triggered by all sorts of factors unrelated to relocation: kids beginning school, midlife crisis (a biggie!), menopause (even bigger), and empty nest syndrome, to name only a few.

There are also natural tension points at various developmental stages of a marriage, such as when the honeymoon wears off, when kids are less adorable and feel like more work, or when your sex life seems to have vanished altogether. In other words, there's a good possibility that many of your dual career challenges—and the fact that you're not discussing them as effectively as you might with your partner—have nothing whatsoever to do with moving.

Even if moving is not the culprit, though, its effect on the marriage can't be discounted. Writes Dr. Barbara Cummings, an American whose doctoral research examined the sociological impact of corporate relocation on the family system, "The conventional wisdom among relocation counselors is that the move acts as a catalyst and brings problems in the marriage or family to the surface . . . Whatever balancing act the family had been able to maintain in the prior location could no longer be sustained during the move."

THERE ARE TWO KINDS of work discussions we engage in with our partners. The first are explorations of professional options from a rational point of view. These are the lazy conversations over coffee or cocktails, when couples talk about what they want to be when they grow up. Professional hopes and dreams dominate these discussions. Can I find work, you may ask, that will fulfill my desire to change the world? Provide intellectual and creative gratification? Allow me to be in control of my day or use my God-given talents to their best advantage? Even after a move, these talks are a nonthreatening way to share, and they can be a lot of fun. No one said you have to give up dreaming just because you've moved.

The second kind of discussion, unfortunately, can escalate into unpleasantness. An example is when your partner shows you the family budget and says if you don't soon find some work and make some money, the family will definitely be going without this or that. Or offers a comment like "So-and-so's wife is making a fortune teaching English as a second language. Why the heck can't you do that?"

This second kind of discussion is seldom constructive. Not only do talks like these often place unreasonable expectations on the spouse (she may be trying her hardest to find work but hasn't been successful, or he's forgotten there's a child at home still in diapers), they also make the spouse feel guilty for not contributing to the family's bottom line. These are no-win scenarios, and I can't tell you how many women have felt as I did, that a job in the new location must be found to silence the husband's money worries.

WORKING SOLELY TO MAKE money was decidedly not the deal I struck with my husband to get me on the plane to Seoul. In fact, it was an arrangement the exact opposite of that which finally convinced me to abandon a well-paying writing contract in Ottawa, pack up the house, and move again barely two years after our previous Asian assignment. I had recently hit forty and experienced all the midlife angst that goes with that. I didn't really know *what* I wanted to do with my life, except that I didn't want to move again. I was not a happy camper.

In order to appease me and satisfy his government masters, who wanted him for the job, my husband suggested our time in Seoul would be a wonderful couple of years for my writing. He promised I'd be able to return to my writing full-time, something I'd never been able to do in Canada, where two incomes were required to pay the bills.

With assurances that an unencumbered writing life would be mine, I was more or less convinced that off we should go, despite my mixed feelings. I realized that I'd be ungrateful if I turned down such a golden opportunity. At the end of the day, it was *his* job that was supporting us. Plus I loved him and didn't want to break up my family. Was there really any choice?

Flash forward to two weeks after our arrival in Seoul. The Korean economy was running great guns at the time, and it turned out there was lots of easy money to be made, not only teaching English (which I didn't qualify to do) but in writing English documents for all sorts of businesses. I'd been doing business and corporate writing for years as a way to earn money. Before I knew it, my full-time creative writing life had vanished under the not-very-subtle pressure to join the working masses.

Weren't all the other spouses working? Think of the money we could save! All I had to do was phone this person or that, and I'd be firmly entrenched in the world of fat paychecks. Canada had a reciprocal working arrangement with Korea for the spouses of diplomats, so a work permit didn't stand in my way. My husband saw Seoul as our El Dorado at last!

Soon, my own writing was something I did in the predawn hours just as I had back home. I was beside myself. Ostensibly, the issue was money, but was it really? I didn't mind making it (who would?), but the deal we'd struck to get me packed up and on the plane was clearly off, and I was mad as hell. Money wasn't the point: my husband had changed our deal. He'd failed to understand that writing for money and writing as an intellectual exercise are two different matters.

While money indeed was splendid, I wrote for the creative fulfillment it provided me with as well as to support and advocate for issues important to me. Buried in all the resentment I was feeling was a lesson about the way I communicated my needs to my husband, one I wouldn't excavate until a few years later (and will tell you about in the next chapter).

THIS BRINGS ME BACK to the different ways women and men communicate. As we've seen, men usually can't listen without offering advice. Even if you aren't looking for advice, and you just want to discuss how you feel about abandoning your career or what you might do next, your husband probably wants you to try this or do that. He's got no end of ideas. Meanwhile, you want him to shut up and *listen*.

Men are very direct, write the authors of *Why Men Don't Listen.* "Men's sentences are short, direct, solution oriented, and to the point, drawing on a broader vocabulary and peppered with facts. They use quantifiers such as *none, never,* and *absolutely.* This kind of speech helps close business deals quickly and efficiently and is a means of asserting authority over others. When men use such direct speech in their social relationships, it often makes them appear abrupt and rude."

And how. My husband came home from a business trip once the night before I was due to leave for one of my own. My trip had required a tremendous amount of preparation. He'd been away for over two weeks, during which time I'd put out the usual household fires, dealt with the children's issues, and tried to write the lectures I was about to deliver on the other side of the world. I wanted to talk about the stress I felt from organizing my trip. He wanted to tell me what I should do. I flipped. "Don't talk to me like I'm one of your employees!" I shouted at him. "I'm the mother of your children!" (A line always guaranteed to secure the moral high ground.) To his credit, he backtracked and realized he'd been too abrupt with me. To my own, I realized I might have let him put down his suitcase first.

"When things get difficult," advises therapist Phyllis Adler, "it's good to know how to stop the argument before it goes beyond limits, to stick to the subject in the here and now, and never to say hurtful things just to score points."

Something else to keep in mind during those career chats: they might bring up old marriage war wounds involving *competition.* Many couples who move around have been dual "fast-trackers" as well as a dual career couple. Both have been chasing after success. Marriage dynamics that have been sustained by competition will require a realignment after a move; and that realignment may not favor the accompanying spouse. If you were tied with or ahead of your husband on the fast track, and the move finds him suddenly speeding ahead, the two of you aren't going to be feeling very good about each other. One of you is becoming more successful than the other, and you're not used to that.

COUPLES NEED WORKABLE DEFINITIONS for the terms they throw around, very often in anger and frustration, in order to communicate in a healthy, not hurtful, way over career challenges. Absolutely everyone, from therapists and researchers to couples themselves, agrees that communication is vital. But without a few semantic ground rules, you and your partner will constantly be talking at cross purposes, and the conversation will go nowhere. So let's put a fresh spin on a few expressions.

Redefine "dual career marriage"

To begin with, I'd like to suggest that the term "dual career marriage" is itself outdated. There's the implication in the phrase that a *non*–dual career marriage must include a partner not engaged in work that's meaningful simply because it is unpaid labor. Furthermore, to assign an adjective like "dual career" to the word "marriage" is to make these marriages sound different from any other kind. Yet in the United States, for instance, 80% of households are considered dual career. So let's throw the term away altogether.

In the context of mobility, if the word "career" is more usefully defined as a "path through life," then a "dual career marriage" might be better understood as a relationship encompassing two unique life paths, both *equally* requiring direction and support (although not necessarily on the same day).

Two people may take turns choosing which path they follow *as a couple,* if the economy or the job market allows such a choice. But over the long term, it's far healthier for a woman to recognize how interdependent the separate paths are, especially during a relocation.

In a traditional marriage, according to Rosanna Hertz in *More Equal Than Others,* "a wife becomes economically dependent on a husband, and he becomes emotionally dependent on her . . . to provide the physical support necessary to continue working (meals, clean clothes, a household) and the psychological and emotional support necessary to withstand the demands of work."

When a marriage is uprooted, it might seem that one path is getting more maintenance than the other. Women often feel shortchanged, since they are typically providing most of the emotional support without getting any back. That fuels angry outbursts and unproductive conversations.

It's not hard to find career counseling these days, but what many women feel they need during a relocation is *life* counseling, and they desperately seek that from their partners. But just as your husband is not your girlfriend, neither is he your career counselor. Trouble can brew when you forget that. Talk to a supportive friend instead or find a professional coach.

Find new meaning in "success"

"Success" is another term that needs to be redefined to fit the ever-changing career landscape, in both the relocating and the non-relocating worlds. With so many married women desperate to leave their jobs to stay at home or do something else, and studies that claim many women who are successful in their careers have never had a chance to pursue family as well ("You Can't Do Both," screamed headlines while I was writing this in 2002), a cynic might conclude that success, in the case of a moveable marriage, simply means a marriage that survives a move. But refer back to that list of positives I suggested you make at the beginning of this chapter and see which side—the positives or the negatives—your list favors.

I did a lot of soul-searching while I was writing this book. One major breakthrough I experienced as a result of my introspection was the realization that I *have* been very successful—as long as I shy away from using money as my measuring stick and also acknowledge the longevity of my marriage. Many of the women I interviewed certainly think of themselves as "successful" (on good days, of course). But they, like me, have adopted the long-term thinking that's required for us to do well (that is, be happy) in the short term.

Redefine your "self"

For mobile women, it's not usually a fear of the unknown that locks them into situations that give them no pleasure. A mobile woman is so used to braving unknown situations that fear has become second nature. For her, the challenge is to figure out what will make her happy, indeed, to know her "self." That's a tough exercise, and one that's easy for her to keep moving to the bottom of her to-do list.

The famous American journalist Dorothy Thompson, writing in the mid-twentieth century, called this exercise a showdown with one's self. "One cannot exist today as a person—one cannot exist in full consciousness—without having to define what it is that one lives by . . . without being clear in one's mind what matters and what does not matter."

Quoting Thompson in her book *When Work Doesn't Work Anymore*, Elizabeth Perle McKenna points out that Thompson was advocating something very relevant to contemporary women: "the need to take . . . stock of where we are, what we like about it and what we don't." What could sum up the situation for mobile women more perfectly?

As McKenna writes, this introspection means that "we have to be ready to switch from the accepted system of recognizable success to something more individually rewarding. It means living by our own values and sometimes that requires substantial sacrifices. But until we make the commitment, most of us find we are stuck in a state of profound inertia, paralyzed by the fact that we're going to have to give something up." Or, in the case of mobile women, paralyzed by the fact that we already *have* given something up.

As Ann Crittenden rightly points out in *The Price of Motherhood*, "For all the changes of the last decades, one thing has stayed the same: it is still women who adjust their lives to accommodate the needs of children; who do what is necessary to make a home; who forgo status, income, advancements and independence."

Too often, women will use that kind of comment to justify giving up. I know, because I've felt like throwing in the career towel on many occasions. Many people believe that two "careers" can't be sustained during relocation, especially if a family includes children. I don't believe that anymore. It's true that someone, usually the partner whose career has not precipitated the move, must learn to adapt, be flexible, compromise, and reinvent. But it should be obvious from this chapter that if you redefine "career," reinvention can be the best thing that ever happened to you.

FIVE

money, sex, and intimacy

One summer evening in Vancouver, I briefed four couples about to move to different regions in Asia on their first international assignments. They were all in their late twenties, roughly the same age my husband and I had been when we first moved abroad. They seemed so young and naïve to me, starting out on both their marriages and their moving adventures with only romantic ideas about what lay ahead. Feeling ancient and jaded, I steadied the bucket of cold water I was about to throw over them with my opening question.

"So, have any of you discussed money yet?"

Their eyes revealed collective shock. Clearly, words of comfort had been more what they were expecting. Selecting one of the husbands at random, I asked him point-blank: "Are you putting your wife on an allowance? And what are you doing about her pension now that she won't be able to make contributions through her job?"

While he squirmed uncomfortably, I turned quickly to his wife—who until that moment had seemed relatively composed—and asked her: "So, how are you going to feel when you suddenly became *totally* financially dependent on your husband?"

No one bolted from the room, but it must have been awfully tempting.

MY INTENTIONS THAT EVENING, and the purpose of this book, were to flag the sticky subjects couples usually don't want to *think* about before they move, never mind speak about openly. These are subjects traditionally discussed only behind closed doors.

not even aware

I want to open the door a crack here, so that you'll know there's not only validity to these challenges (again, you are *not* going crazy) but that predictable patterns crop up in most marriages, moveable or not. So please stop worrying if shouting (yours) or pouting (his) has been going on about any of these issues in your home.

In the context of relocation, staying balanced in the three mainstays of marriage dynamics—money, sex, and intimacy—can be tough. These issues are negotiated differently during the course of a move and relocation. A series of trade-offs and deals is often necessary to bring everyone on board and keep them happy. For instance, I've met women who've had money thrown at them by their partners to pacify them (this was never our scenario, sadly). Then there are the scores of women for whom even the *word* "money" raised in connection with their partners can make their blood boil.

"I'm now financially dependent, which doesn't bother my husband but bothers me terrifically," thirty-eight-year-old Jane wrote to me. "As much as he doesn't want to admit it, he does feel he has more power since he makes the money. So now we have to contend with those issues along with everything else."

Every couple at some point fights over money, sex, and intimacy (and in-laws, too, but that's a whole other story). That is, unless the wife is a visitor from a planet of independently wealthy Amazons, capable of unpacking a thousand moving boxes by day and transforming into a sex kitten by night. Personally, I hail from planet Earth, where most women worry periodically about money and, at the end of a long day of unpacking, settling children in, and feeling isolated, lonely, and unemployed, deliberately ignore all signals (raised eyebrow, room full of candles, naked man—pick one) initiated by the person on the other side of the bed.

"There's an old adage in war that 'truth' is the first casualty," says counselor Dr. Barbara Cummings. "My observation is that in relocation, the couple's sex life is the first casualty. Anger, exhaustion, and a lack of communication all play a part."

Therapist Phyllis Adler says she's often surprised at the number of relocated couples she sees who don't have sex at all for different reasons, many of which remain unknown because men don't typically join the discussion on the subject. (I hope, though, that they are secretly reading their wife's copy of this book.) "Sex is supposed to be an expression of a positive relationship, but it's also used for a myriad of other reasons," Adler cautions. "I think it's good to keep in mind that we are not taking 'ideal' marriages and moving them. These are people who often just happen to get moved—warts and all— and then find the move makes the warts grow."

Whatever trade-offs or compromises a couple comes up with, they will never entirely eliminate power struggles or fights for control at the bank or in the bedroom.

Financial arguments usually are over how money will be spent and who's going to control the purse strings. In the case of physical intimacy, another power play is in motion.

Talking about any of these subjects creates tension, but so does avoiding them altogether. Nor does it help matters when a woman decides to go on a spending spree with a credit card to "get even" or when an accompanying spouse decides she'll control the only agenda she can, namely the couple's lovemaking schedule.

Once again, finding a way to communicate is the only thing that will help you and your partner sail through these stormy waters.

I'll get back to sex and intimacy in a minute, but first, let's talk cash.

UNLESS THERE'S GOING TO be a money tree planted in the back garden of your new digs, you and your partner need to start discussing financial arrangements the minute the move looms on the horizon.

As a start, ask yourself this: how well do you know the state of your family finances? Can I be the first to admit that when my husband shows me mortgage tables and convoluted explanations of principal and debt, the page goes blurry on me? But if you've tended to leave the whole nasty business of money in your husband's hands, now is the time for that to change. I've certainly decided to take a more active interest in our family finances. Researching and writing this book—and recognizing that I wasn't taking my own advice—was a wake-up call I have started to heed.

"The spouse should be involved in *all* financial planning during a relocation," advises Tom Boleantu, a professional financial planner based in Calgary, Canada. "If the spouse doesn't insist on this, then she is at risk. She shouldn't delegate the planning to her husband."

When advising couples about to move, Boleantu emphasizes that both parties need to attend tax and financial planning sessions prior to their departure. "It's cheaper to hire a babysitter so you can attend a financial planning session than to risk losing it all," he says.

The U.S.-based Institute for Equality in Marriage worries that too many women, whether mobile or not, are dangerously uninvolved in family finances. "There can't be a strong *we* without a strong *me*," according to the institute's website, *www.equalityinmarriage.org*, which suggests a variety of ways that women can become more knowledgeable. "To achieve true equality in a partnership, both individuals must have knowledge of and involvement in their partnership's assets and debts . . . If you currently aren't involved in your partnership's finances, look for ways to become more integrated in that part of your marriage . . . Sharing responsibility can be rewarding and make your partnership more balanced and fulfilling."

The institute's mission should resonate with corporate spouses. It was founded in 1998 by Lorna Wendt, after her very public divorce from the former CEO of General Electric Capital. Wendt, offered only 10% of the family's assets by her husband, decided to fight back and defend her role as an equal partner in their long-term relationship. With some of the money she won in her settlement, she started the institute.

"My case was never about the money," Wendt says on

the institute's website. "It was about someone implying I was a ten percent participant in my partnership. In reality, I always gave 100 percent, putting my career on hold to raise the children, manage the household and support him in his business endeavors." Ring any bells?

MONEY GURU AND AUTHOR Suze Orman, in her many self-help finance books, stresses the need for "financial intimacy" in relationships as well as emotional closeness. More importantly, she believes that grown-ups need discretionary income. "Sharing is important in marriage, but so is autonomy," writes Orman.

This idea of discretionary money leads to a subject some women would rather die than discuss or engage in: the possibility of being given an allowance after a relocation. The word alone sends chills down many women's spines.

Receiving an allowance may be a practical solution, but it does nothing to alleviate the stress of a spouse feeling she has to go to "Daddy" for lunch money. Some spouses find they adjust fairly quickly, especially if the allowance is generous and they aren't forced to keep returning for handouts to purchase books or lipstick. But when the allowance isn't sufficient (and the working partner dips into the family bank accounts at will), the stress can plunge a spouse into what I call *allowance hell*.

Not everyone ends up there. Diane wrote to me that she and her husband, who have made multiple moves, have no his/her accounts. "Frankly, there's not enough to divide!" she admitted. "But anyone is free to spend as they wish. Neither of us feels the need to have or to spend excessively. Emotionally, money means different things to me than to my husband. We're aware of and respect those differences."

For couples who decide to use the allowance scheme, settling on an amount for the spouse's spending money is often a major roadblock. Anecdotal evidence (including my own experience) confirms that most men don't know the price of anything.

"It has been humiliating having an allowance," twenty-nine-year-old Alice, a relative newlywed, wrote to me after an international relocation. "My husband has no idea what imported books cost, or maybe he thinks that things from home aren't important. We constantly fight about how much I spend on everything, from food to my own books and supplies . . . It's hard knowing it's not 'my' money I spend, and I feel like I have to hide things from him so he won't know how much I'm spending and on what."

Setting the terms of the allowance is insulting to many women, but even worse when, as in the case of Mary, a thirty-seven-year-old mobile wife, the husband is "tight-fisted with money." She wrote: "This coupled with the fact that I never got comfortable with not earning my own money was a huge problem. His idea of an allowance was a pittance. I haven't felt so poor since college. Now that I'm working again, we are getting along much better."

THERE ARE QUESTIONS EVERY woman should ask in order to learn the particulars of her partner's pay package, since these are often not fully disclosed to the accompanying spouse. For one thing, these matters are almost always handled at headquarters, through company intranets, or in meetings with the Human Resources department, so the spouse learns about them only secondhand. It's wise to read the employment contract that spells out the allowances and compensation your husband is to receive at home or abroad. Keep in mind, too, that many of these packages include compensation or reimbursement for professional training programs for the spouse, information that may not make it out of your husband's briefcase without prodding.

Pension issues are particularly difficult. If a spouse has had to leave her career behind, it's probable that her pension was left behind as well, or at least her ability to make contributions to it. Likewise, without the spouse's regular paycheck, the couple's ability to contribute to other investment vehicles for retirement may not be feasible unless this prospect is discussed in advance, preferably with a financial adviser.

Many spouses relocate during prime earning years. What is the working partner doing to compensate for that fact? Nonworking spouses, if they are smart, will seek financial advice (with the full knowledge and cooperation of their partner, if possible) so that the family's books are wide open and retirement or investment funds are not abandoned. Spouses can't ask for the impossible, but once they know what financial resources are available, and some goals are set, realistic budgets that cover the spouse's day-to-day life at the new location, as well as money to be set aside for the future, should be worked out.

MEN WORRY ABOUT MONEY the way women worry about weight. With one major difference: for men, there's never enough of it; for women, there's always way too much.

This is a fact of marriage that women must accept and learn to handle.

Two years after our last move back to Canada, my own frantic job search led me into a disastrous business venture and the job I mentioned earlier writing for funeral industry magazines. Both left me demoralized and insecure, and I realized I couldn't take the pressure anymore of finding satisfying work that would contribute to the household accounts *and* allow me to serve as the frontline parent while my husband traveled for his job. We'd examined our budget over and over again, and I was so tired of feeling angry and guilty that one day I reached my breaking point. Here's what I did.

I told my husband I would reduce my personal economic needs to zero. (Except for professional hair color four times a year—I'm not completely crazy!) In return, I would become a "born-again spouse" and do it all, short of meeting him at the airport in a negligee. Much better for our marriage to do most of the unpaid labor around the house without a murmur than to greet him upon return from his road trips with a loaded pistol.

I explained I wanted the freedom to write another book; to volunteer for community service, mostly at my children's schools, because this was important for all of us; and, most of all, I wanted to get him off my case. An amazing thing happened: something snapped inside of him. He heard (for the first time, I believe) the frustration in my voice and he went along with my scenario. I quickly settled into writing again. My secret hope is that as I follow my heart, the money will naturally follow. I'm still waiting for the money, but I'm breathing a lot easier these days, and our marriage has survived. Of course, it helps that I've started playing more golf with him, too.

Our decision seems to be working out well, although we still circle around it from time to time. For example, on occasion I've told my husband I wanted a full-time job, but I immediately recant the minute a child is sick and he is away on business. Being out of town when I take back my words, he always misses that part of the conversation, and for a few days he returns constantly to his initial position of wanting me to work outside the home and make money. The pressure tactics begin again, always couched in language like "But you said you wanted to work!"

I'm married to an extremely generous man who has denied me nothing, supported my writing life, and is the world's best husband and father. I love him dearly. He's the family accountant by my own choice, and he carries the burden of all the bookkeeping paperwork. (This, by the way, was a mutual decision after I forgot to pay our property taxes.)

As I mentioned earlier, I'm starting to pay more attention to our family finances. Ultimately, though, my partner decides how we spend "our" money, since he's the breadwinner and I'm the full-time mother. When he shows me our financial records and tells me how much we can afford to give ourselves in spending money, I'm left with little choice but to comply. My wants are modest (although a new computer would be nice). And he rarely spends money on himself. Even so, the idea of someone controlling what I can spend sometimes drives me nuts, and many other women, too.

IN EVERY MARRIAGE, A PARTNER learns how to push the other's buttons. The money button has a giant x on it, as if it could possibly be missed anyway. Throw a relocation into the mix, and the money button shares a place of honor with that other popular marital retaliatory tool: sex.

On a holiday from our life in Beijing, our entire family stayed at a posh resort in the Thai tropical paradise of Phuket. The location was extraordinarily beautiful, hidden on a private cove, with so many amenities you didn't have to leave the premises. A magnificent swimming pool was the centerpiece, and that's where we decided to park ourselves during the day. For me, it meant the kids (then eight and four) could splash around within my peripheral vision. For my husband, it meant an unadulterated view of topless European female guests, many of whom, as I pointed out to my young daughter, were boasting surgically altered upper bodies. I never noticed their faces. I'm sure my husband didn't either.

The daily soft-porn parade poolside definitely had an effect on him. Or maybe it was the tropical air floating around the bodies beautiful. Whatever the reason, he was awash in holiday mode. Before we'd left Beijing—a hardship posting—we'd discussed how we'd try to do as little as possible on our holiday. More importantly, we'd promised each other that neither of us would pressure the other to do anything he or she wasn't keen to do. (I did relent once to go whitewater rafting, for fear of never seeing my young son again.)

Anyway, it happened that, early in our stay, the Academy Awards were being broadcast on Thai television. Since I was a movie buff, and had been deprived of television and cinema for many months (this was long before satellite TV became accessible, and at that time videos couldn't be rented in China), the awards ceremony was something I was really looking forward to watching. Unfortunately, my husband had something different in mind. He wanted the television turned off, since he was feeling "romantic."

I was stunned. I pointed out that if a football game had happened to be broadcast by some miracle, he would have killed me if I'd turned it off. Needless to say, I missed the broadcast in which Kevin Costner picked up several statues for *Dances with Wolves*. In our hotel room (with the children safely asleep in the room next door), yours truly was playing the role of Dances in a Very Bad Mood.

WHEN A SPOUSE FEELS out of control in her life and her marriage, it's not uncommon for her to seize one part of the relationship in which she can claim the upper hand. Some wives control the kids (as I'll discuss in the next chapter), but others set the timetable for sex. This fact may not be openly articulated (there's that polite conversation rule again), but it happens everywhere, whether consciously planned or not.

Withholding or constantly acting disinterested in sex because someone is controlling your money, and indeed every other part of your life, may seem like a great idea in the short term. But it's obviously not a long-term, viable solution for a happy marriage.

And there are other serious issues, often emotional ones, that can get in the way of sex and have nothing to do with the love you feel for your husband. They have everything to do with how you feel about yourself—which as any mobile woman knows, at the beginning of a relocation, can be pretty lousy.

A WOMAN'S SEX DRIVE is significantly affected by events in her life, according to authors Barbara and Allan Pease of *Why Men Don't Listen.* "If she hates her job, she has a really demanding project at work, the mortgage payments have just doubled, the kids are sick, she was drenched in rain, or the dog ran away, sex will not even be a consideration. All she can think about is going to bed and sleeping.

"When the same events happen to a man," continue the authors, "he sees sex as a sleeping pill—a way of releasing the built-up tensions of the day. So at the end of the day, he puts the hard word on the woman, she calls him an insensitive moron, he calls her frigid, and he gets to sleep on the couch. Sound familiar?"

Oh yes. There was a time when my husband was traveling excessively, even for him, and once when he returned I felt compelled to ask him: "Do you really come home from these trips to see me and the kids? Or just for clean shirts and sex?"

More to the point for our purposes, a woman's depression over the relocation—and many women feel tired and depressed for months, until they settle into a new groove—will negatively affect her physical relationship with her husband. When she's depressed, a woman isn't going to feel like "connecting" with her mate, or with anyone else, for that matter. People suffering from depression often isolate themselves from loved ones, and this situation is no exception.

Part of a woman's depression on relocation may come from her struggle to establish a new identity. There may be an undercurrent of anger as well.

"Without a clear 'I' we become overly reactive to what the other person is doing *to* us, or not doing *for* us—and we end up feeling helpless and powerless to define a new position in the relationship," writes Dr. Harriet Lerner in *The Dance of Intimacy: A Woman's Guide to Courageous Acts of Change in Key Relationships.*

"Selfhood," or simply no loss of "self," is an important key to a woman's feelings of intimacy, Dr. Lerner firmly believes. "But when anxiety is high, and particularly if it remains high over a long period of time, we are likely to get into extreme positions in relationships where the self is out of balance and our relationships become polarized," she writes. I often wondered while reading her book if she'd been a fly on my wall.

INTIMACY, LOVE, AND SEX. Those three words are kissing cousins, closely related but not one and the same. Sex often doesn't involve love; love doesn't always need sex to validate it. Intimacy is close to love but different. Together, love and intimacy enhance a physical relationship.

But what *is* intimacy? In my opinion, it's a key element in regaining balance after a power struggle over money and sex. And if intimacy can be re-established after a stressful relocation, it can save the day.

Intimacy is often described simply as an emotional closeness or bond between two people. As any couple who has relocated knows, it is precisely that lack of closeness a woman misses most. She feels shut out of the new world her husband has entered, while her own new surroundings are still alien. She's desperate to feel connected, especially to her husband. If a couple can work towards feeling close again after a move, it will have a positive impact on almost all aspects of their married life.

"An intimate relationship is one in which neither party silences, sacrifices, or betrays the self, and each party expresses strength and vulnerability, weakness and competence in a balanced way," according to Dr. Lerner in *The Dance of Intimacy*. "The problem arises when we confuse intimacy with winning approval, when we look to intimate relationships as our sole source of self-esteem."

NOT SURPRISINGLY, WE HAVE come full circle back to self-esteem. The better a woman feels about herself, the more likely it is she will feel confident and ready to live her entire life to its fullest, including her married life.

Recovering self-esteem, one of my recurring themes, is the biggest challenge facing a woman who moves to a new city or country because of her husband's job. Strong feelings of self-worth are required before she can comfortably walk out the door to find paid employment or make new friends, and these feelings are essential to keeping her relationship strong. Husbands reading these pages, take note. Help her feel better about herself, and you'll probably get lucky again.

In defense of males, Dr. Lerner points out that men are up against both gender-based and historical challenges. "Men often feel at a loss about how to become experts on close relationships, although their anxiety may be masked by apathy or disinterest," she writes. Moreover, "many men have been raised by fathers who were most conspicuous by their emotional or physical absence, and by omnipresent mothers whose very 'feminine' qualities and traits they, as males, were taught to repudiate in themselves . . . Finally—and perhaps most significantly—males are not rewarded for investing in the emotional component of human relationships."

In other words, it's up to us, ladies. Let me get the ball rolling with a few ideas surrounding money matters and intimacy that have worked for me.

Plan budget meetings

When any couple, mobile or not, sits down to review finances, there is often tension in the air. But this tension is aggravated in relocated marriages by the costs associated with moving into a new home. Decisions about buying everything from new appliances and a car to salt and pepper shakers can be made in the same breath and on the same day. Money flies away, depleting bank accounts in a matter of hours. Budget discussions can be especially stressful when a mobile wife is months away from contributing to the family bottom line. Harsh words may be exchanged, tears may fall, and the meeting may dissolve in a sea of bad feeling.

Plan your budget meetings carefully, paying close attention to the amount of time you devote to them. Belaboring issues that create stress is not helpful. You can counteract the tension by doing something fun together immediately afterwards. Make reservations for a nice lunch or dinner, or take a relaxing walk. In other words, put the discussion in its place and try to move forward.

Share your financial histories

Since we all carry baggage into our relationships from our childhoods, there's a good chance that our family financial histories may be contributing to present-day tensions. For instance, the way you make decisions about spending money may be eerily reflective of the way your parents did. The idea of an allowance may bring back money memories that are having a negative effect on your relationship.

Growing up, I had an extraordinarily generous father who compensated for the loss of his wife (my mother) by throwing money at me and then saying afterwards: "What, you *spent* it?" Those mixed signals issued by the breadwinner carried over into my own adulthood until I opened up and discussed my experience with my husband.

Likewise, if you grew up living within limited means and then for a few glorious years were financially independent in your chosen profession, married life—especially a relocated one—can bring back those years of *wanting* in a flash. Does your husband know and understand this? Talk to each other about money and the ways it has been used and abused in your past.

"Screw you" money

I was forty years old before I had my own bank account in my marriage. Of course, I had managed my own money when I was single and working, but I was always engaged in creative accounting as I juggled credit card debt, car payments, and the thousand other things I used to spend money on before marriage made me fiscally responsible.

But for my fortieth birthday, I insisted at last on my own account within our marriage. My new bank account did not have to do with buying anything in particular. It was about giving me the ability to spend money without pre-authorized clearance, the part of our relationship that always drove me crazy (and many other women I've spoken to as well).

My "screw you" account isn't terribly polite-sounding, but its meaning couldn't be clearer. This is *my* money to spend as I see fit or give away to a worthy cause of my choice.

Golf plays well

When I tell the men in my audiences that golf saved my marriage, their glassy-eyed expressions disappear, and they suddenly perk up and pay attention. What is it about golf, anyway?

The reason I highly recommend golf to women is this: as long as you've made it clear that there'll be zero tolerance for temper tantrums on the course, golf can be one of the most relaxing, nonconfrontational ways to be with your husband, even when circumstances have created a tremendous distance between you or you're carrying a load of anger or resentment. You simply *can't* say much on the fairway other than to ask: "Did you see where my ball went?" or "How much club are you going to use?"

But golf is really just a metaphor for any leisure activity in which couples can engage together to feel close. I prefer golf because it takes place outdoors in pleasant weather and—unless you're one of those people with the gall to carry a cellphone on the course—you'll have four or more uninterrupted hours with your mate.

BEING A JOURNALIST, NOT a therapist, I've only scratched the surface of the highly charged emotional challenges money, sex, and intimacy create in a marriage. If financial planning, finding new ways to communicate, and giving each other respect and space don't work, it may be time for professional intervention. Please don't hesitate to seek it out. These challenges can be "deal-breakers" in any marriage, and never more so than when they are magnified by a relocation. Don't let these problems fester.

SIX

parenting

Like most new mothers, my dog-eared copy of the parenting bible *Baby and Child Care* by Dr. Benjamin Spock was bookmarked at the section on "diarrhea." We were living in Thailand with a new baby daughter, after all. With my head stuck in the section on baby bowel movements, I never bothered to search out Dr. Spock's advice about moving with children until years later, when I was trying to understand our son's negative reaction to his first relocation.

The world-famous pediatrician didn't live to see the impact of globalization or the emotional and physical strains on parents forced by economics to move their children to faraway locations. Otherwise, he surely would have offered more words of wisdom for couples coping with the havoc created by transplanting a young child into unfamiliar surroundings, and warned them about the impact this could have on their marriage.

Avoid introducing change into the life of a two-year-old if possible. That's the gist of Dr. Spock's sadly limited advice on the matter. Unfortunately for the peace of our household, our son, Jamie, had just celebrated that magic age when we moved him from Canada, where he was born, to Taiwan so that his father could study Mandarin. His older sister, easier with change and happier by nature, made a new friend immediately and never looked back. But Jamie was unsettled by the shock of moving from clean, crisp, convenient Canada to a city of smelly drains, narrow alleys, and parents who seemed to have shed their personalities and become screaming monsters. It's no coincidence that turned out to be the most difficult year of our marriage.

Jamie chose to demonstrate his discontent at the top of his little lungs. My own voice was not much calmer. My husband and I were hanging onto our sanity by a thread.

That move was particularly fraught with tension for a number of reasons. Primary among them was the fact that we'd been hung out to dry by my partner's employers, who wanted to test-case a Canadian foreign service officer living in Taipei. We had insufficient support on all fronts, especially for a family with a two-year-old child in tow.

Trying to make the best of a bad situation, we agreed to take turns looking after Jamie. My husband tried to memorize the extremely difficult Mandarin characters while his son played with Lego at his feet. At other times, over on the other side of our cramped apartment, I drafted my first book with Jamie sitting on my knee. He loved playing with the computer keys—including the "delete" button—because it was such fun to watch his mother become hysterical.

I lost my temper with my son constantly during that year. And my anger wasn't simply over losing precious text from my computer. (I could do that very well without his help.) My stress over the move, heightened by our lack of support, was always simmering below the surface. That meant the most minor of incidents could set me off on a rampage, whether it was aimed at one of my children, my marriage partner, or some innocent bystander.

I wasn't proud of my behavior, especially after hearing my son's early attempts at language come out sounding as salty as my own. He was very talented at mimicking my vitriol from the back seat of our car as I drove him down the narrow Taipei streets. On the day I barely missed driving over a dog lying in the middle of the road (the animal was already dead, as it turned out), my son came out clearly with his first four-letter word. I was thrown even further off-balance by that. My husband got an earful of my own choice four-letter-words as soon as I got home.

How my partner managed to learn Mandarin in the midst of all these temper tantrums is a feat I still hold in utter awe. I came out of my own language classes with barely a memorable word, and that was without an unhappy toddler to distract me.

My husband and I look back at Taipei as the rockiest time in our relationship. Jamie's inability to adjust to his new surroundings led to more shouting matches, more hand-wringing and recriminations over the idea of mobility and, indeed, over my husband's choice of a career in the foreign service than we've weathered before or since.

CHILDREN REQUIRE PARENTAL STABILITY to feel secure about their lives. Yet consistency and balance in the parents' relationship are two elements sorely lacking during and following a move.

Mobile parents have needs, too, but these are usually sidelined in favor of the children's. Among other things, adults require a modicum of peace and quiet to let the stresses of the relocation lift. There's no way that's going to happen with an ornery toddler or a truculent teenager in the house. In either event, it's almost a certainty that the already high levels of stress involved in parenting are going to shoot through the roof during relocation, with a predictable filtering through to the marriage.

Following a relocation from one part of her country to another, Australian mother Janice wrote me to say that, after being on the move as a family for over twenty years, their last move had been the "hardest all round." For the first time, Janice managed to make the connection between a child's unhappiness and the rough days her marriage was undergoing.

"All our moves had been relatively easy on our children, and so there had been no obvious pressure on our marriage," Janice wrote. The problems in their last move started when one child left the nest for university, leaving a young daughter of fifteen (never an easy age, under any circumstances) in a new city without her older brother. The younger teenager found it difficult to break into new friendships and was angry with her parents for making her leave the comfort of home.

"I thought I was coping really well until our daughter went away for a week and my husband and I were alone without children," her mother wrote. "I was finally relaxed, and even my new friends noticed and said I looked the happiest I had since arriving in our new home. Until then, I hadn't realized that my husband and I had not had any time to ourselves. Our time had been entirely preoccupied coping with our daughter and getting her through the settling-in period—which is still continuing. It's obvious to us now that her behavior had been encroaching on how we felt, but I wasn't aware of the deep effect it was having on us both until she was taken out of the equation."

After a move, relationship stress can also be intensified by the frustration of discovering that your child's education will be seriously disrupted in your new location or that medical needs can't be met easily. Many women become virtual single parents, with husbands either constantly on the road or always stuck at the office. Other parents, especially those moving to international locations where having a maid is common, worry about raising children with a heightened sense of entitlement. These tensions are universal for mobile couples, and so too are the ways they impact on both your children and your marriage.

UNFAIR ACCUSATIONS ABOUT WHO'S responsible for unsettled kids are commonplace and can trigger quarrels between partners. For instance, a woman accuses, surely her husband, the employee, is to blame for the problems their kids are encountering. Of course, that's only part of the picture. But as with all the other challenges created by relocation, it's convenient to lay the blame for everything at the employee's door.

Your child won't fall asleep? Well, obviously, it's because he's been moved to another city or country! He wouldn't be experiencing any of this otherwise, right? Or so you will claim—worry and sleep deprivation can make even the most loving of mothers grasp at such dubious notions. And who has the energy to be fair when you are exhausted and a toddler or teenager is driving you around the bend?

But the fact of the matter is that no one person is to blame. Criticizing only each other—or the company or the child—often means the partners are not willing to accept their own culpability. Taking some personal responsibility is a good first step towards finding workable scenarios to help everyone carry on as best they can.

It's not only the needs of very young children that create stress in a moveable marriage. As children hit puberty (I tend to gloss over what I think of as the "golden years" of five to twelve in which kids begin school, still generally enjoy their parents' company, and aren't too challenging to handle), the stresses can hit your marriage with a bang. The mood swings of a teen, let alone one angry about being moved, will have an effect on your entire household.

Deborah, from Australia, a veteran of more than a dozen domestic moves, felt as if she and her husband had failed their son because he was forced to repeat a grade after "falling through the cracks" during the emotional lead-up time to their last relocation. "After much agonizing, our family came to the conclusion that our fourteen-year-old son would be best served repeating the eighth grade," she wrote to me. "This was an extremely difficult decision, for with this conclusion our family (and that would mainly be me and my husband) had to confess to some problems we would rather pretend hadn't existed in our recent relocation. We were so caught up in our own 'relocation drama' for the better part of nine months. My husband left first, and I stayed behind to sell our home and cars and everything else. In the meantime, my kids were left to fend for themselves." Stress over the move and her son's avoidance of studying, never his favorite activity, combined to end up in a failure at school.

The happy ending to this story is that a parental lesson was learned. Deborah and her husband acknowledged their own responsibility for creating the situation. "During our discussion with our son, we tried to emphasize the truth, which included our own shortcomings in the situation. Our approach was well received, with promises from our son to be more focused in the coming year, while my husband and I vowed the same to our son."

I've always subscribed to the role-modeling template for good parenting, whether at home or on the move. Unfortunately, children don't always show discrimination in their choices of parental qualities worth emulating. It's terrific when they adopt those character traits you admire most in yourself, yet positively terrifying when the bad ones get taken up along with the good.

Badly handled stress definitely falls into the latter category. We don't come off looking great to our children when we're fighting with our partners. Worse, we can easily transfer that stress onto our kids, who may not be feeling exactly secure themselves.

This is especially true after a relocation. Eyeballing their parents at the evening meal as the adults pass jibes along with the potatoes, children will soak up the tension along with the gravy on their plates. Uncertain or nervous themselves after a day at a new school or one with a new caregiver who may not even speak the same language, they look to their parents as their rocks of stability. A dinner scene that starts with sniping between the parents can end in a nasty bunfight that engages the entire family.

"Sit up straight and eat your meal," a spouse irritated with her husband may snap at a child whose only crime has been to push his vegetables to the side of his plate. That kind of behavior only fuels bitterness and anger between the parents (you know the drill, "Leave him alone, it's *me* you're mad at"), and pretty soon, the whole situation has disintegrated into unpleasantness, with everyone's unhappiness throwing oil on the fire.

There's only one unarguable truth in all of this: family dynamics will shift as a result of relocation, and that shift will impact on your marriage. Your family is experiencing a unique form of shock after a move. The relocation has precipitated it, but it could have been caused by any other major life change: an illness, a divorce, or a death.

"Family culture shock is a *collective* experience," I wrote in my earlier book *Culture Shock! A Parent's Guide.* "It is initially about loss of control over new surroundings and then, later, over each other's behavior. As each person struggles with the shock of regaining equilibrium, the traveling family's culture shock also includes feelings of losing control over the actions and reactions of the other family members. Factor in conditions like constant physical and emotional proximity in the early weeks, and family culture shock can't help but produce confusing, unsettling interaction."

Relocation throws families into flux, and it takes time and considerable patience to allow life to settle down into a new routine. There are many steps parents can take to make their families feel comfortable with each other in their new surroundings, and I offer some of these at the end of the chapter.

For now, just remember that if work is done to get the family back on track, tense marriage dynamics will ease up, too. By the same token, "getting a marriage back on track will help the family," therapist Phyllis Adler says. "In their focus on parenting, too many couples with young children forget to take care of each other. There needs to be a sense of balance."

THE DIVISION OF LABOR within the family, always a sore spot between partners, can become a particular flash point during a relocation, particularly if the working partner's job requires his absence a good chunk of the time. That popular "who's doing more" standoff travels with you.

In the cheekily entitled *The Bitch in the House,* a hilarious collection of essays about women, marriage, and motherhood, contributor Hope Edelman, though not mobile herself, debunks "The Myth of Co-Parenting" in a way that will surely resonate with a relocated spouse.

"It began to make me spitting mad, the way the daily duties of parenting and home ownership started to rest entirely on me. It wasn't even the additional work I minded, as much as the total responsibility for every decision made. The frustration I felt after researching and visiting six pre-schools during my so-called work hours, trying to do a thorough job for both of us, and then having John offhandedly say, 'Just pick the one you like best.' *I didn't sign up for this!*" writes Edelman.

"John would say he'd be home at eight . . . but forget

to call about the last-minute staff meeting that started at six, and when he'd walk through the door at ten I'd be too pissed off to even say hello," she continues. "Instead, I'd snap, 'How much longer do you realistically think I'm going to put up with this crap?' And the night would devolve from there . . . Both of us were stuck on that crazy carousel, where the more time John spent away from home, and the more pissed off I got, the less he wanted to be around."

Whether they are traveling or at the office, the places many mobile fathers aren't appearing are at the dinner table, a child's sports event, or that musical at school, not to mention parent-teacher meetings.

One of the worst scenarios for a mother just moved to a new place is fearing her husband will be incommunicado even if there's an accident of some sort. In fact, therapist Phyllis Adler says that one of the breaking points for women with children can come when they have to fill in the phone numbers on a new school form. "When they can't provide emergency phone numbers— no neighbor and especially no husband who can be reached easily—it scares them and makes them feel even more isolated and angry with their partners, for putting them and the children into the situation."

Exacerbating family culture shock further, a mother —incensed over the financial dependence she's fallen into—sometimes runs out and grabs the first job on offer, before her children are comfortable in their new surroundings. Then neither parent is keeping the home fires burning, and the cracks are there waiting for a child to slip through.

No matter where you move, there's no escaping the

work-and-family balance conundrum. Women are still in charge of the domestic sphere of the marriage (home, kids) while the husband goes off to fulfill his economic destiny. This separation of responsibility is more pronounced during a relocation, certainly in the early days. When children's needs are not met, they will feel lost and do what kids normally do to show unease: use their behavior as a means of getting attention. That rarely involves using their *best* manners, and parents start tearing their hair out over them and each other.

IT'S A WELL-DOCUMENTED FACT that the arrival of a new baby, the source of so much joy for couples, also places enormous strain on a marriage. It's not just the shock of feeling totally responsible for the needs of another person. It's often the redirection of attention and the complete absorption (to the exclusion of each other's needs) that comes with a new addition to the household.

Many couples who move internationally take the opportunity, as we did, of starting their families in countries where relocation offers not only lavish housing but live-in help to keep the place running. That includes the care and feeding of new babies. But believe it or not, even this can cause stress. There's not a woman I've met who didn't have a power struggle with a caregiver at some point, even if she was lucky enough to have affordable help.

When a baby is born during a relocation, its parents are far away from the extended family members who traditionally guide couples through the early days of baby shock. New parents who are freshly relocated are left to their own devices. This can be helpful in building self-reliance and independence in the new mom and dad, but overwhelming on bad days, when a grandparent's soothing intervention with a child would be most helpful.

Some relocations may involve affordable caregivers waiting in the wings to carry the baby off to the nursery. (That was certainly the case for us when our daughter, Lilly, was born in Bangkok. Our wonderful Thai caregiver, Suporn, happily became Lilly's personal "handmaiden" while continuing to do the drudge work for us.) But at the end of the day, a caregiver is not a parent, and the situation can often *heighten* a mother's sense of isolation from her own mother or other family members she'd normally have around to help her. Trying to discuss her feelings with her husband may create tensions too. Not unreasonably, the hard-working employee may ask: why is she complaining about his absence when she has a house full of help?

Clearly, a new baby creates emotional confusion from all directions. Couples have to stop to ask themselves honestly: What are we fighting about, anyway? Are we fighting about the mere presence of a new baby? Are we feeling isolated without our own mothers here to help us? Are we stressed out because we can't find the right doctor or a certain kind of diaper? What's causing us to turn a joyful event into a disaster in our relationship?

If new parents can identify the underlying reasons for their tense feelings (which may also be due to the unfairly balanced workload, as in the non-relocating world), they can begin the work to ease exhaustion or soothe hurt feelings and move on to adoring their bundle of joy.

OUR BABY DAUGHTER WAS barely six months old when

my husband decided her parents needed a holiday—without her. This was not fueled by a desperate need to get away from her, since Lilly was an easy baby from day one. It was about allowing the adults to spend quality time together after sharing such a life-altering event.

We decided to take a holiday in New Zealand. I'm using the euphemistic "we," of course. Despite a desperate craving for clean air, dairy products, and lots of roast lamb (none of which could be found in Bangkok at the time), the last thing I wanted to do was leave my baby behind in a foreign country while I swanned off for two weeks to the ends of the earth. As a journalist, I could already picture the headlines announcing the crash of our plane en route, and the stories that would note in tear-inducing detail that "one young Canadian couple had just had a baby." An overactive imagination combined with fear of flying can be dangerous.

My best friend in Bangkok, another Canadian expat who'd had a baby girl at the same time, encouraged me to take the trip with my husband, even offering to look after Lilly while we were gone. "It will be good for your marriage," I can remember her saying. I was still apprehensive, even though I knew I'd be leaving Lilly in the best of hands.

The holiday was all about my husband's need to have time alone with his wife. The same issue might have come up back home, but it provides a perfect example of how an ordinary challenge becomes magnified after a move. In our case, since we'd moved to a foreign country, it seemed foolish not to take advantage of traveling in that part of the world. (Believe it or not, on a map it looked as if Thailand and New Zealand were not too far apart. Were we wrong!)

Caught between my baby and my man, I decided to go with the man, although not without giving him some serious hassles en route. As you may have guessed, I'm a bad flyer to begin with, and the idea of leaving my baby unnerved me so much that I started drinking vodka way too many hours before flight time. My husband certainly got his holiday, but not before he had to dispose of several barf bags used by the Passenger from Hell sitting next to him.

My husband and I chose to look after the needs of our marriage first, even though one of us wasn't comfortable with the idea. Other parents faced with this same challenge will do what feels right to them. Both my husband and I had positive childhood memories of our parents going off for wonderful winter vacations without us, and that helped. Once I got over my hangover, we had a great trip Down Under. And when we got back, our daughter was just fine.

THE WORST SCENARIOS AFTER a family move can often be for parents of children with learning disabilities or special needs. The difficulty of finding new medical resource people or special education can create serious tensions in the marriage. A mother frantic over her child's unmet needs may throw all of her frustration onto her partner and his company or organization, especially if there are broken promises of company support. The result can be emotional exhaustion.

Cheryl and her husband, Sam, accepted an international assignment involving both their careers. "I loved my job," Cheryl wrote to me. "I worked hard and worked my way up in the ranks of the company. I had only known work (I started at a very young age) and had never thought I would do anything else, or indeed want to do anything other than my work."

But upon moving to the new location, Cheryl and Sam discovered that one of their young children had a disorder requiring a specific form of occupational therapy. Once they'd tracked down someone who could provide it—no simple matter—the child's appointments forced Cheryl to give up her job. She was devastated. "When I resigned, I'll be honest and say I didn't feel I knew how to mother or just be a wife. I never wanted to be a stay-at-home mother."

Worse, having worked side by side with her husband in the same company, she had attended meetings where the men groused about their spouses. "When I quit, I remember thinking that now I was going to be one of the wives they were complaining about. I knew I'd given up a great job, but who was going to take our daughter to her appointments?" Matters worsened when her husband started staying out late with colleagues from work and told her he was tired of listening to her complaining. Cheryl fell into depression.

Fortunately, this story has a happy ending. After experiencing the lack of resources for parents in her new community, Cheryl and a friend started a nonprofit group designed especially to provide support for parents who found themselves in similar circumstances. And, more relevant to their marriage dynamics, Cheryl discovered that her husband was actually prepared to help out with their daughter. She just hadn't asked for his help, expecting none to be forthcoming. "When I started inviting his input, instead of shutting him out by assuming he wouldn't help me, he stepped up to the plate every time," she says.

FEELINGS OF GUILT FOR moving a child are among the most common stresses in a moveable marriage. The father feels guilty that his job necessitated a relocation; the mother feels she must be at fault for not saying no to the move and protecting her children from change.

Guilt creates circles of anger and resentment between partners and the arguments begin, centered on a child's behavior, an environmental illness that has cropped up in the new location, or a learning disability that has surfaced since the move. It doesn't matter what the issues are, the end result is blame being thrown back and forth. Kids are caught right in the middle, and they start to fight back in their own way, acting out or hiding in their bedrooms.

Sometimes, a child cottons on to the shift in power in the marriage and begins to seek out the parent who holds it (the breadwinner) to ask for material goods and exotic trips or simply for permission to stay overnight at a friend's. If honored (and they too often are, by a traveling parent wanting to assuage his guilt), these requests can create more intense power struggles between the parents.

FROM ALL OF THESE variables, an alarmingly dysfunctional family and marriage may emerge. This doesn't always happen, of course, but the potential is there. It's for this reason I've been red-flagging some of the issues that parents caught up in their "relocation dramas," as the Australian mom expressed it, very often don't see or choose to ignore.

As adults and heads of the family, you and your partner bear the responsibility for setting the family boat right. Your children have often not moved voluntarily, and that goes a long way towards explaining the anger they feel at leaving friends, sports teams, and familiar surroundings behind.

The good news is that many mobile families have successfully weathered these challenges, even turning them upside down to create a family that is closer thanks to a relocation. You'll have your own ideas about how to do this, but to get you started, here are some specific measures you can undertake.

Research the new location and environs

I've written three previous books and numerous articles about the culture shock of mobility. In my opinion, the more you know about the challenges associated with transition, the better everyone in your family will handle it. Yet I've had people tell me I'm overpreparing women and ruining the exotic adventure of jumping off a cliff into a new life in the great unknown. I understand the sentiment of leaving some things to fate, but the question here is really: Do you want to jump off a cliff with a two-year-old without either of you wearing a parachute?

There are enough surprises in store for your children, not the least of which will be the personality changes they perceive in their parents in the midst of a move. The *last* thing they need are more shocks or broken promises. Parents who do their homework about new locations—and that can sometimes mean taking kids to see the new house, new school, new playground, and new mall before you actually make the move—will find that when children can picture themselves in a new place, the fear of the unknown will lessen. Your children can even write to a child in the new location if you set it up with other parents there. When they feel calmer, so do you. A little research will go a long way, and thanks to the Internet, it's never been simpler to do.

Keep children and their father in touch

E-mail has been nothing short of a miracle on many fronts, but it's especially good for keeping traveling fathers in the family loop. Children love getting and sending funny notes and stories through cyberspace. E-mail is a handy way for spouses to communicate as well. With more and more videoconferencing being used in business, it won't be long before this too will be a tool that allows an absent father to stay in touch.

Establish new family rituals

Family rituals and customs are touchstones for children. If your family has some already, make every effort to continue them in your new location. Establish new ones, too, even something as simple as playing a card game every Saturday night or sitting down for dinner together on Fridays or Sundays. Rituals, religious or cultural, are all about helping people feel a sense of belonging. Family rituals also help reinforce a child's sense of security.

Learn to say no to your children

Children aren't stupid. If they know their parents are guilt-ridden or out of sync after a move, they'll see that conditions are ripe for manipulating their elders. As parents, you must learn to say no. Full stop. From the standpoint of your marriage, however, make sure both of you agree to say no *first*, or one parent's efforts will be undermined by the other.

Should you stop moving?

In speaking to groups of parents who have moved around the world, the question I'm asked most often is, when is the best time to stop moving children? Couples everywhere fret and fight about this. But it's a hard question to answer in a general way. Each couple and every family will have different needs and opinions.

"I feel personally that moving is basically not good for kids," Karen, an American foreign service wife, wrote to me. "I have a six-year-old and a ten-year-old, and while I don't think either of them are 'scarred for life,' I don't see that the benefits have outweighed the disadvantages." The family will be moving home to the United States soon, and they plan to stay until both children are out of high school. "That time frame is a compromise between myself and my husband, who grew up moving around," Karen wrote.

Clearly, the operative word there is "compromise." Rather than let the wife's feelings about the effects of relocation on her children gnaw at her insides, the couple has decided together to take a break from mobility.

Family counseling

If you've come to recognize that your family is in serious trouble, please take the crucial step of finding a therapist (family, marriage, or both), and the quicker the better.

Many family counselors do double duty as marriage counselors, so one therapist may meet all your needs. Shop around until you find a professional who will make family members feel comfortable enough to spill their guts and can get the entire family on board for counseling sessions. Don't let anyone in the family off the hook.

IT'S DOUBTFUL MY HUSBAND and I would have been such proactive parents if his job hadn't required constant relocation. Nor do I think my nuclear family unit would be as close as it is today without the mobility that was the hallmark of our children's early years.

There's no denying that the stresses of parenting have been magnified by our many moves and my husband's constant business travel. Many of these stresses have led to some unhappy interactions (an understatement) among all of us. But at the end of the day, yet again taking that necessary long-term view, relocation has had a positive impact on our family and our marriage. We have become a tight unit by facing challenges collectively as a family. We've learned to enjoy each other's company immensely, without relying on outsiders to entertain us. And as parents, my husband and I are much more involved in our children's lives than we would have been if we'd stayed put.

SEVEN

when a moveable marriage
goes wrong

It's handy that one of my older brothers is a divorce lawyer, if only for its deterrent effect on my husband. Luckily, I've never needed his professional services, although I've called him many times to obtain generic legal advice for a relocated spouse. Laws governing divorce differ around the world, but the necessity for a woman to know her rights, preferably before she leaves home, crosses all borders.

Unfortunately, not every woman has an advocate standing by when there's a marital emergency such as infidelity or abuse. And if she's moved to a new city where she may not know a soul, or somewhere where the language is different, her isolation can be frightening. When her marriage is in trouble in a new town, a woman doesn't know where to turn for comfort or assistance.

The gossipy nature of international communities can also make it much harder for a woman who discovers her husband has been fooling around to stay cool and in control. Many women worry about traditional routes such as counseling, because of fears that speaking to *anyone* about the situation will somehow reveal family secrets in a tight-knit community.

Even more distressing, a woman may be married to a man everyone in her community thinks is a great guy, while in reality he's emotionally or physically abusing her, their children, or both. Abuse happens more often than most of us want to contemplate or talk about openly, which can make a woman feel even more isolated or, worse, think she's going crazy. The cycle of domestic violence in a marriage does not break just because a family's location has changed, and in some cases a move away from extended family and friends can exacerbate the situation.

Facing terrifying violence at the hands of her partner is every woman's nightmare come true. Please seek immediate assistance if you find yourself in this situation. I've listed some resources at the back of this book that may help, including an online "virtual" shelter for American women overseas.

UNFAITHFULNESS IS HARDLY A new story in modern marriage. But as with most marriage tensions increased by relocation, it's more difficult for a woman to handle when she's on her own in an unfamiliar setting. Among other practical considerations, if a woman has to leave a marriage that's been mobile for many years, she may have to start over financially without marketable, up-to-date skills, in addition to no longer having a home.

The sheer number of stories about adultery circulating in highly mobile communities demonstrates there's a strong perception (and a legitimate worry, too) that many moveable marriages are in the kind of trouble that will eventually end up in divorce court. There are various reasons for this reality.

Some men can get "just plain stupid" (in the words of women who wrote to me on this subject) when they are promoted to a new job, accept a short-term assignment away from home, start working a commuter job that requires being away from home all week, or become road warriors, traveling constantly for business. These are all work scenarios that can create a climate for adultery, and I take a closer look at them later in the chapter.

When they are trapped in a 24/7 workweek or doing hard time on the road, some men find it's very easy to guide nature into taking its course. This may be especially the case on international assignments where an employee works and travels with an attractive colleague who isn't whining all day about the loss of *her* career or the company's latest broken promise. And if an employee is treated like His Excellency on the job, with minions to do his bidding, it's not hard to see how a sense of entitlement about engaging in an affair could follow.

Of course, wives play their part in this drama as well. They, too, initiate adulterous affairs. And who among us has not taken our husbands for granted? The line for the guilty forms to the left.

INFIDELITY ABROAD IS FREQUENT and is very often the man's, according to Jeremy Morley, a British lawyer working in New York City and founder of *www.international-divorce.com.* "Everything is suddenly different for him," says Morley. "The new location is far more exotic than 'home,' which may have become mundane; his daily routine is often refreshingly different; his work is more interesting and, as a result, he feels more interesting and alive than before; and he feels special because he receives unusual attention, especially from women.

"But in the evenings, when he returns to his home in the new city, he finds the same wife and kids and the same old issues, as well as some new ones related to overseas adjustment. His wife does not treat him like the interesting, youthful, and special person he felt like at work. Instead, she's been dealing with the kids who have no friends, hate the new school, and can't stand the food. Or she's bored and meets no one except some other wives who are also depressed. She can't wait for her husband to come home so that she can complain to him and have him share in some of the household chores. The contrast is stark, so he prefers to spend time at the office, and that eventually leads to an affair."

Marriage counselors hear some amazing rationalizations from men for their adulterous behavior. Here's my all-time international favorite: "This is one way I feel I can connect to the local culture."

Usually, the reasons for infidelity are more mundane. "I've worked with men who feel like they are just a meal ticket for their wives," says therapist Phyllis Adler. "The man doesn't feel very appreciated." Different values are also at work. "Some men truly don't know how much it can hurt their wives if they are unfaithful, because it doesn't mean anything to them," Adler says.

MANY MEN THINK MONOGAMY is what furniture is made of, write authors Barbara and Allan Pease in *Why Men Don't Listen and Women Can't Read Maps.*

"Human males fit the specifications of a polygamous species; it's no wonder that men have a constant battle to stay monogamous. Promiscuity is wired into a man's brain and is a legacy of his evolutionary past," they write. "The reality is that men, like most primates and other mammals, are not biologically inclined to complete monogamy. We live in a world that is completely different from our past and our own biology is often completely at odds with our expectations and demands."

Not all experts agree. In *The Seven Principles for Making Marriage Work*, Dr. John Gottman draws on data gathered in his "marriage lab" at the University of Washington in Seattle to explode common myths of marriage breakdown. He believes the evolutionary, or "law of the jungle," theory of adultery is off base. "Whatever natural laws other species follow, among humans the frequency of extramarital affairs does not depend on gender so much as on opportunity," he writes.

A hotel room on a road trip, a short-term assignment, or any other work arrangement that keeps a husband away from his family can certainly provide ample opportunity. A global working world does indeed create a climate in which adultery can flourish anonymously. Even in settled couples, there are always marriage partners who feel the pull towards an affair, but opportunity knocks more often in the mobile world.

Many accompanying spouses are left behind in a strange new city or country when the working partner's job sends him on the road before he's stopped to catch his breath or unpack a single moving box. It's not as if the travel happens without warning. Most women know in advance, rationally, that their husband's new job will take him on the road, especially if it's in a regional location with wide territory to be covered.

But the *emotional* reality often doesn't really hit

a woman until, one fateful day, she looks at the family calendar hanging in the kitchen. Week upon week has been blocked off for a parent who's going to be away (not her), and those weeks often coincide with major family events such as birthdays, anniversaries, school plays, the dog's rabies shots, season tickets for the symphony, or a dinner date with friends that's been rescheduled so many times all hope is lost of ever getting together.

Compounding a woman's emotional exhaustion is the household version of Murphy's Law: if something is going to break down in the house, it will invariably break within twenty-four hours of her husband's departure. And as every mother knows, children save their worst viruses for the moment the airport taxi has left with their father in it.

As a result, a man who travels a lot on business is often leaving behind a woman who feels very irritated with him. He may be upset with her, too, maybe at her lack of support for his work. Off he goes to be with people who *do* appreciate what a great guy he is and, what's more, a female co-worker who thinks he's attractive— and so an affair begins.

WHENEVER I MAKE MY cynical observation about feeling like a single parent without dating privileges, I'm guaranteed a hearty laugh of recognition from my audiences. My partner, however, gets downright snarly upon hearing it.

"Quit using that line already," he has scolded me on many occasions.

"But it's true, and you know it!"

I certainly *feel* single with him away so much. I'm restless and bored, especially when he's gone over several weekends. I usually resort to movie therapy (renting a stack of movies and holing up by myself with a bushel of popcorn in our basement television room) to stave off my loneliness for adult company. Or worse, I end up working when I should be taking time off from the computer. In the early days of our relocations, I felt abandoned and hopelessly insecure for weeks at a time.

never!

It is this emotional insecurity that marriage therapists say leads many women into the arms of other men.

Annie's story is a perfect example of how women may fall into a relationship outside their marriage when it was actually the last thing on their minds. Like many women who indulge in an affair, Annie didn't deliberately go looking for an opportunity to be unfaithful to her husband. It happened one day when she was sick of being alone all the time.

"I would never have believed that I could have an affair," she wrote to me. "I was, and continue to be, in a good marriage despite the lack of company and verbal communication when he is not around. My husband, while traveling a lot, always shows his love for me and our children when he is home. I was almost appalled by the fact that I could have strong feelings for another man. It was such a shock to me."

Annie's story is typical of many other women who decide to stray. When she began her affair she was angry at her partner, not only for his business travel but because he'd started talking about another relocation for his career just when she was beginning to feel settled again.

"I felt powerless to openly express my anger over the idea of being uprooted again, because it would have made matters worse," wrote Annie. "He really wasn't being given much choice about the move, and for my part, I felt I had no voice in the discussion. I felt really hurt that he wouldn't take my feelings about moving again into consideration, so when I met someone who would listen to how I felt, things just got out of hand."

Fortunately for Annie's marriage, her family moved and the relocation put an end to her flirtation with adultery. She sought therapy and learned a few other things worth sharing.

At the time of her affair, Annie was in her late thirties and, without realizing it, was heading into the stage of her life when many men and women begin re-evaluating the choices they've made in life. In particular, Annie was having second thoughts about choosing to marry someone who would keep her moving all the time when she felt ready to stay in one place for a while.

And like many other women who wrote to me as they approached the terrifying age of forty, she felt unattractive and worried she would never experience romance again. She'd become depressed over the life transition to middle age. Luckily, working with a therapist, Annie managed to separate out her issues and move on with both her life and her marriage.

THANKS TO THE SHORT-TERM assignment, the latest corporate staffing brainchild, there are spouses who don't have a clue when their partner is going to return home. The short-term assignment typically begins as a six- or twelve-week job but not uncommonly turns into six months, a year, or even longer. These assignments have started to crop up more often as companies realize they can avoid the expense and challenges of posting the employee's spouse and family by simply not relocating them in the first place.

At first glance, this may seem a reasonable human resource solution for both a company that needs an employee in a new place and a spouse who doesn't want to abandon her own life and career or uproot children. But in a temporary assignment without limits (or with time frames that keep shifting), companies ignore the new set of problems they are creating at home. Household life turns upside down for the spouse who stays back (who may also hold a full-time job), and the domestic routine is only made worse by an employee who comes home on leave and expects the household to stop and entertain him.

Some of these challenges also hold true for marriages in which one person commutes between home and a job, whether that job is halfway around the world or in the next province or state. Once again, this arrangement solves personnel problems for the company while creating other problems at home. Many families accept these situations because there is no choice, especially if children want to remain in schools with their friends or with special education teachers they wouldn't have access to otherwise.

Although it's certainly true that absence can make the heart grow fonder, it can also harden the hearts of even the most loving couples. Long separations are unhealthy for any relationship.

Phone calls can turn nasty if the working partner happens to phone home precisely at a family zero hour. Dinner has just been put on the table, or the woman is rushing out the door with children headed for soccer practice or a music lesson, or she's engaged in any number of activities for which she now carries the full burden of scheduling and transportation.

For this reason, I've discovered, many men actually dread making the call home. An interesting article I came across one day, written for business travelers, reported how men worry incessantly about what time they should phone to check in with their spouses from the road. Should they do it as they are walking out the door to dinner? Right after they check in to the hotel and really want nothing but to take a shower? Late at night when they might sound half-comatose? The challenge, it seemed, was to hit a time when no one at home was going to be busy or upset by the interruption of their phone call.

I thought this telephone fear was positively hilarious until I mentioned it to my husband. He shuddered and said, "Oh yes, *the call*." I got the message loud and clear. Now we mostly e-mail each other unless he's traveling in a country where he can't get online. I realized *I* would hate catching me at a bad time, too.

PAULA'S HUSBAND HAD BEEN on assignment on his own for eight months when she discovered his infidelity. They had moved eleven times internationally and domestically to support his career. Paula had once worked in the same industry but left to follow him. She admitted there were signs their marriage was in trouble long before she officially ended it. Many of the challenges she pointed out to me in our correspondence confirm the themes of earlier chapters, such as money and power struggles. Paula is also quick to point out her own culpability.

"I don't imagine it was a picnic for him to live with me, since I essentially changed the ground rules when I found my voice and began to put up resistance to always doing things *his* way. He was used to calling all the shots."

When it came to the assignment that eventually ended her marriage, Paula didn't initially join her husband, so he was there for eight months before her arrival. Finally, she made the decision to join him in an effort to stay in the marriage. It was her second marriage, and she was hopeful it would work out better than her first.

"I think he would have been okay with my not moving overseas to be with him the last time, but life was such an upheaval when he came home on leaves. I preferred to make the move and not have these regular interruptions to contend with. He didn't adjust well to the idle time of being on leave but not on vacation somewhere exotic, to my still going to work every day, to his friends not always being available to entertain him while he was in town.

"When I moved to be with him, my spouse kept insisting that he was never unfaithful, but it didn't feel right to me—his reactions to innocent questions were not on the level. His behavior and reactions didn't add up right, so, deep down, I knew. It turns out that he *was* seeing someone on the side, and once I had positive proof of that, I made my plans to leave."

Did they consider marriage counseling?

"He refused to go to counseling. Part of his unwillingness to go, I believe, was that he might have to confess he was seeing someone. He denied it until I had a love note in my hand that he had written to someone else."

Since Paula wasn't sure she wanted to stay in the relationship anyway, the note presented her with a timely invitation to leave the marriage. "I was thrilled, actually, because in the end, the decision I had fretted over for so long, through so many moves, was now so easy to make! I think he was a little shocked at how swiftly I made my departure."

Ironically, Paula believes that one of the reasons the relationship lasted as long as it did was *because* of all the moves. "I could focus on re-establishing our home again (and all the settling in) and not dwell on the problems in the relationship," she wrote to me.

Nowadays, after taking two years to resettle herself, become employed again, and make a new community of friends in her home country, Paula focuses on the positives to come out of the divorce and the many relocations she made during her marriage. "I moved *way* outside of the sheltered environment in which I was raised and learned to appreciate and accept people from different walks of life and cultures. My horizons definitely expanded."

NOT ALL WOMEN LEAVE a marriage after trust has been broken. Laura was shattered to find herself in a new country with her two young children when she discovered bank deposits made by her husband to a woman unknown to her. He confessed to the infidelity when she confronted him with the evidence.

"It was devastating to me," wrote Laura. "I was in a foreign country, no credit cards or cash in my name, no way to leave the kids without my husband's permission, middle-aged with no job prospects. I was profoundly scared. For the first month, I emotionally bounced between feeling numb (with lots of eating and some drinking) and huge rages and sobbing. I had suicidal thoughts. I spent a lot of money out of anger."

Yet, two and a half years after she discovered the bank deposits, she remains married. "I believe all marital problems can be worked out," she says. "I would definitely have left if my kids were in danger, but that wasn't the case. He's a good father and he loves our kids dearly. We both wanted to actively heal the marriage, and while time doesn't heal all wounds, keeping our marriage intact was good for the kids. But effort and change from both partners are necessary as well."

THERE WERE NO CHILDREN involved in the marriage that ended overseas for Alice, a thirty-something American woman. Working in the same industry as her husband, she had found a good position while he was still searching for a job. That didn't sit well with him. He turned to substance abuse, and it wasn't long before he became abusive with her as well.

"My own moveable-marriage story is a particularly horrid one," Alice wrote to me. "I was not expecting to be so violently homesick, nor was I expecting my spouse to react so violently to that homesickness by screaming and shouting at me, then going out drinking when I couldn't stop crying. This only increased my sense of isolation."

A negative pattern emerged for them. "I was the one who 'acted out' our mutual homesickness, while my ex maintained that he was never homesick, not one bit."

While he spiraled into drinking and drug use, she pulled herself together and got on with her new life.

"My ex seemed to be crashing further and further, hardly leaving the house, doing drugs, blowing several job interviews, and bringing home strange people whom I suspected of being drug dealers. When I challenged him on this, he became physically threatening to me and I had to leave the house. I already felt emotionally abused."

Alice returned to their home and dragged her husband to a couples therapist to try to patch things up. But in the end, she decided to leave him. "My recipe for trouble was that one of us wanted to get out and explore and the other wanted to just stay at home, watching American TV shows."

She feels only sadness when she looks back at the beginning of their time abroad, when she and her husband were still enthused about their boldness in making a move and their new life together.

Alice admits she wasn't perfect and had unrealistic expectations of her husband. "Yet I feel that our isolation as a couple was exacerbated by his substance abuse and that he was using substances as a way of avoiding dealing with me. Skeptical as this may sound, I would advise any spouse relocated overseas to have enough money for a ticket home, an emergency place to stay in your own country, and control of your passport and other important documents."

FACED WITH AN ABUSIVE husband, Alice was lucky she happened to be living in a country that provided her with access to resources such as battered women shelters and lawyers, a place with a cultural awareness that domestic violence is unacceptable. This was certainly not the case for Paula Lucas, the courageous founder of American Women Overseas. The safe website she established, *www.awoscentral.com*, serves as a virtual shelter for American women abroad who are victims of abuse. Her organization also provides a twenty-four-hour international crisis line, with the telephone number posted on the website.

Lucas went from living a comfortable expatriate lifestyle in Abu Dhabi in the United Arab Emirates, with servants to look after her three sons and a thriving international marketing firm, to camping out in women's shelters across the United States. She was fleeing from an abusive marriage that she's the first to admit no one around her even suspected.

"Nobody wants to know about domestic violence," says Lucas. "It's as if society at large thinks if nobody talks about it then it doesn't exist. Being abused abroad is even worse than at home since it's a double-jeopardy situation for expatriate victims. While living abroad, they fall under the jurisdiction of the laws of the host country, and those laws inhibit their embassies from helping them. Too often there seems to be this mentality that 'she should have known better in the first place than to go and live in a foreign country.' This attitude is ignorant. Abuse occurs at all levels in societies. Abusers abuse because they can get away with it."

Based on her own experience, Paula Lucas created the website, which sadly has no shortage of visitors. "I modeled AWOS on what I wish had been available for me and my children when we were victims of domestic violence.

Expatriate life can be lonely, but imagine being abused when your husband is further isolating you from a society that doesn't have any domestic violence resources available even if you did dare to seek help. It can be a desperate situation.

"Most of the e-mails we receive are frantic cries for help, and often the women are suicidal. In fact, we are often told by a woman contacting us that she feels the website was God's intervention. Most are suffering from 'battered women's syndrome' and others are suicidal and have no hope left. The only typical thing about each situation is the level of desperation the woman has reached."

Many expatriate women living in foreign countries are afraid to report their abuse or that of their children. But although they often especially fear going to the police or their embassies, according to Lucas, this is one of the most important things women should do.

"It's critical that women not delay documenting the abuse," she says. "Otherwise, when they go to their embassies after a very severe beating and are truly fearful for their lives, their government representatives will say: 'This is the first time we have even heard of it.'"

Even so, foreign embassies often tell a woman they can do nothing because of an absence of policy on the issues. That's why Lucas is also working to establish domestic violence "protocols" in American embassies so that there is a system in place for women to report the abuse.

What can multinationals or other organizations that relocate families do to help? Carrie Cuthbert, who runs the Women's Right Network, a human rights organization based at Wellesley University outside Boston, believes that education about domestic violence should be mandatory for all company staff, including CEOs. Company employees need to know that domestic violence is a global and cross-cultural violation of women's human rights, according to international human rights laws and norms, and they also need information about the relevant laws in each country where the company has a plant or office. As Cuthbert points out, domestic violence has direct impact on the company's bottom line, and employers have a clear and calculable stake in addressing it. Cuthbert believes that companies should also have international protocols, through Employee Assistance Programs, for handling situations where an employee is either a victim or a perpetrator of domestic violence.

As for Paula Lucas, it took her seventeen months of legal battles before she was awarded full custody of her children. Her ex-husband is allowed to see them only under the supervision of a family facilitator. He continues to deny any abuse, which the experts say is typical for batterers.

THERE ARE MANY PRACTICAL and legal steps a spouse can take to protect herself in case her marriage goes wrong. Here are some ideas to consider.

Hope for the best but plan for the worst

According to international lawyer Jeremy Morley, it pays to plan for an unexpectedly bad ending to your love story. In the case of overseas assignments, for example, he feels it may not be wise to sell a house before departure.

"If you maintain an address back home, it will be

much easier to claim you maintained your home as a permanent residence," Morley says. "Keeping your family home will also make it much less traumatic if you need to return to it, and will also make it clear to a court that the home is needed for the woman and her children."

My family-lawyer brother, Ottawa-based Lawrence Pascoe, believes that it's important for a woman to have money in her own name that she can access in an emergency, to cover things such as retaining legal counsel or buying a ticket home for herself and her children. Credit card advances are one way to access cash in a hurry; a line of credit at the woman's disposal is even better, advises Pascoe.

Make a postnuptial agreement

Both Morley and Pascoe believe there is also value in having a postnuptial agreement in place before a relocation takes place.

Given the extraordinarily high number of marriages that end in divorce, it's neither unrealistic nor cynical to relocate a marriage with eyes open wide about the possibility that it could end. For a woman giving up her ability to make money, in particular, an agreement will provide some certainty before she leaves home that compensation will be forthcoming if things don't work out as planned.

What *is* a postnuptial agreement? Most people have heard of prenuptial agreements, but far fewer are familiar with postnups, according to the Institute for Equality in Marriage. The institute is a major proponent of these agreements for marriages in general, but I see a direct application for moveable marriages in particular.

"Even if you have been married for many years, it's

never too late to enter into an agreement that promotes domestic harmony and protects your union," the institute states on its website. "In fact, veteran lawyers say the number of mid-marriage agreements has exploded in the past five years, perhaps as much as tenfold. There are many negative connotations attached to the word 'post-nup,' as if it is admitting your relationship's defeat. It is less intimidating to look at the process as a communication tool and a 'seat belt' for your relationship in the case of death or divorce."

A postnuptial agreement can give a woman certainty about the support and assets she is entitled to upon separation, says Lawrence Pascoe. "Securing an agreement in writing—besides acting as a potential deterrent on her partner—could also save her having to argue about it later if the marriage does indeed break down during the relocation. She will know before she even leaves home what her compensation—at a minimum—is going to be for throwing her life upside down. A postnuptial agreement outlines a woman's general rights and her husband's obligations if the marriage breaks down."

The resources for a woman to professionally retrain in her field are also significant, Pascoe believes. "The contract could spell out the minimum amount of time and money a woman would get in financial support so she can retrain, especially if the marriage broke down because she moved and sacrificed her own career for her husband's. Even an acknowledgment that she is entitled to retrain would be helpful for many women."

Postnuptial agreements should not be drawn up at the last minute, without legal representation or full financial disclosure, or when the partners are under duress, such as during the last days before a move, according to Pascoe. "The contract should also not be conditional on the cause of the breakup, on who is at fault, or on who wants the split; otherwise, a husband could be having an affair but not want to separate."

How enforceable are these contracts, given that relocations cross state and provincial lines as well as international borders?

According to Jeremy Morley, a postnuptial agreement is not enforceable in an English court but is valid in many other jurisdictions, including the United States. Even in England, though, he says the courts will use it as evidence of the intent of the parties. "In any event, a good agreement may well provide a wife with infinitely more protection than no agreement," says Morley.

Pascoe agrees. "If no contract is in place, it may be that the laws of the country the couple relocated to will apply. Any agreement should specify which jurisdiction governs the separation. Regardless, if there is a contract, it will play an important role in any separation."

Custody of children seems to be the one area lawyers say can't be agreed upon before a relocation, as that will depend on the court in the jurisdiction involved. Most jurisdictions will not allow the parties to decide custody before they separate, and the court will decide at the time what's in the best interests of the children.

Contract or no contract, both lawyers stress the importance of women knowing their rights and obligations. "A woman should take charge of her own case. She shouldn't allow lawyers to make decisions without her full knowledge and complete involvement," says Morley. "She should do her research, ask all of her own questions, and demand intelligent and detailed answers."

"Relocating women are simply more vulnerable," Pascoe believes. He ought to know, since I've been plying him with questions on the subject for over two decades now. "Not only do they not have easy access to a lawyer or to money, but they are surrounded by their husband's workers and friends, not theirs. It's my perception, at least, that the divorce rate is higher in relocation than for those who stay home."

How to raise the subject of postnuptial agreements? "A change of circumstances (financial or lifestyle) can present a good opportunity to bring up the subject of a postnup," according to the Institute for Equality in Marriage. Clearly, a relocation qualifies as a major change in lifestyle. Here's some other advice from the institute on broaching the subject with your husband.

- Approach the topic from a collaborative viewpoint. For example, if you or your spouse is a stay-at-home parent, focus on the need to address your respective contributions to the relationship.
- State your concerns in a straightforward fashion. Be sure to solicit your spouse's input and feedback.
- Remain open-minded and be prepared to make compromises in the negotiation.
- Your financial planner or lawyer could raise the issue in conjunction with your overall financial planning.

Open all the envelopes

When things in the marriage are not working out and there is no agreement in place, a woman must start looking at every document or piece of financial mail that arrives at the door. It's important to know what assets and debts your partnership has. In particular, watch for mail from insurance companies, credit card companies, banks, and courts. Read any documents you are asked to sign, including tax records, and *never* sign a blank form. Make photocopies of everything you sign.

It also pays to visit family safe-deposit boxes and make a list of the contents. Consider renting your own safe-deposit box for storing valuables and important papers. If you're considering divorce but still living with your spouse, rent a post office box or have a trusted relative or friend receive your personal mail.

Finally, make copies of every important document in your marriage, from bank statements to wills to children's birth certificates, as well as documents showing household, child-related, and personal expenses.

Jeremy Morley calls these activities "collecting all the dirty laundry," but he advises women never to threaten a husband with specific information gathered about off-shore accounts or safe-deposit boxes. "A woman will have more negotiating power if her husband knows only generally that she has all the evidence," he says.

Morley has more advice for women whose husbands have strayed and then come home again. "Frequently, I've seen cases where the husband will come to a point, at least temporarily, where he sees the errors of his ways and begs his wife for forgiveness and promises to be loyal, faithful, and honorable for the rest of his life," says Morley. "This is the point where a wife has to be sure she wants him back but should be smart about the distinct possibility that he might not keep his word. It's great to kiss and make up. But make sure you get his promises on the record. In divorce cases, evidence in writing is of infinitely greater significance than promises that were verbal. So if he promises something, a woman should get it on paper sooner, not later."

Never rely on the company for help

It should almost go without saying that one place a woman needn't bother turning for advice in a moveable-marriage meltdown is her husband's company. By their actions (that is, neglect), most employers already reject the idea that family support is crucial to a successful relocation. They are in even deeper denial about marriage problems. They just don't want to know about marriages going bad, even if their actions have been a contributing factor.

From the marvelous website of therapist Peggy Vaughn (*www.DearPeggy.com*), which is devoted to helping women get beyond a husband's affair, come these comments about companies and their attitudes towards unfaithful employees. Vaughn is writing about office affairs in particular, but her observations are relevant to this discussion, too. Her website includes a Beyond Affairs Network that gives e-mail addresses for women's support groups.

"The most subtle and most pervasive reason companies don't take action in dealing with office affairs is that there is no separate entity called *the company;* there are only individuals (usually men) in positions of authority," writes Vaughn. "And many of these men are either involved in affairs themselves, or are close personal friends with other men who are involved. Either way, they are less than eager to 'rock the boat.'"

No one wants to think about a marriage going bad. Marriage contracts were not even legal in my home Canadian province of Ontario until the 1970s, because people wanted to hope for the best and not contemplate the worst. Today, divorce statistics are too high to ignore. They must surely harden even the most optimistic of souls entering into marriage.

In the final analysis, I must stress—yes, again!—that women need to take responsibility for their own lives and not depend on a company or their husbands. *There are no victims here.* That remains the unofficial mantra of this book, written to validate, inform, and ultimately empower accompanying spouses in getting their needs met.

And lastly, remember this: Men don't even *think* about this stuff, never mind talk about it. It's going to be up to you.

EIGHT

restoring balance in a moveable marriage

With each new move my family made, our unpacking ritual remained the same. Boxes were unloaded from the moving van; numerous pots of coffee were made and polished off. Then, as if on speed, my husband and I would tear off the rainforest's worth of paper protecting even the most useless of objects, including those shipped by mistake. Once, we unpacked the fake coals of a decorative fireplace taken from a rented apartment. Another time, the vegetable bins from the refrigerator were thrown into our boxes—which must have shocked the new tenants when they first brought in groceries. Whether we were moving into an apartment in Bangkok, a diplomatic compound in Beijing, or an assigned house in Seoul, we always ran the same race. How fast could we put everything back together again to form the semblance of a home?

Once that was done, we would sit back, take in our new surroundings, marvel at our remarkable unpacking skills, and, before too long, get into a heated debate over something stupid. While we easily discovered the appropriate cupboards and closets in which to place our belongings, we conveniently overlooked finding the right spot for our feelings. Everything was in its new place except our marriage.

Like any new home, a moveable marriage may require a few renovations to make it comfortable to live in. *A marriage isn't like water.* It doesn't pour neatly into whatever vessel is set out to contain it. A few metaphorical walls may need to be knocked down and put back up again, in a different place. The contractors for the job are you and your husband.

WORKING TO RESTORE EQUILIBRIUM in your relationship is essential after your marriage has been thrown off-balance during any stormy transition. Equality, a particular kind of balance, is imperative to strive for in a marriage that is constantly thrown off-kilter by relocation.

"I see equality in marriage as two human beings coming together to form a partnership," says Lorna Wendt of the Institute for Equality in Marriage. "They value each other in rights and responsibilities and are equal in everything. It's not just about finances."

Equality doesn't mean each partner has to be responsible for taking out the garbage 2.5 times a week. "It just means individuals know and appreciate that both parties bring value as a person to the marriage," says Wendt. "Perhaps most important, people need to talk about these things."

Australian Yvonne McNulty, the mobile spouse/researcher quoted in earlier chapters, agrees couples need to discuss the equality—or inequality—of their marriages. But first, she feels, must come a significant measure of self-awareness for women.

"I'm only just starting to understand that I've probably

been my own worst enemy for many years," Yvonne wrote to me. "I want equality, but I've learned that the way I go about getting it is often self-defeating. I doubt myself and my abilities because I'm not earning money. I insinuate things that are not there because my identity gets lost in each relocation. I don't take things at face value, and instead look for hidden meanings in our daily discussions to substantiate my feelings of inadequacy."

Yvonne has learned that equality is often a state of mind, and talking about it with her husband is better than bottling up her feelings inside for months on end. "When I strive for equality, what I'm really after is respect. I want to be respected for my contribution, respected for my efforts, respected for my talents and abilities outside of the paid workforce. When my husband's actions and words demonstrate to me that he has respect for all of the things I do outside of a paid job or career, then I feel equal."

Who among us doesn't want respect from our partner? I certainly want it for the thousand and one things I do (out of love, not for cash) to keep my own mobile family members' lives functioning smoothly. Fortunately, my husband tells me—and often—that he couldn't do his job outside the home if I didn't do mine inside it. He certainly couldn't travel the way he does, nor could any of the married road warriors he nods to in airport lounges around the world. Their wives are also back home taking care of family business.

That's not to say my husband doesn't also encourage and support my writing. After all, could there be a better sport than someone who lets his behavior be thrown around in print and over the Internet the way he does?

He bends over backwards to keep our partnership balanced and equal.

My partner is scrupulously fair in balancing the significant chunks of time he spends away on work-related travel. When he's home, he gives full attention to the children. He stocks up the freezer, too, because as the family cook, he actually freezes meals for the kids and me to eat during his longer trips. (Yes, I already know he's rare!) And my needs, usually for time away by myself, are always a priority for him. When I have opportunities to travel abroad to lecture on the subjects of my books, he's the first one to suggest an extra stopover somewhere, even for a quick holiday on my own. Perhaps that's his guilt speaking, but I hear it as an attempt to redress the travel imbalance.

Do you think your marriage is equal? Stop for a moment and contemplate that. It's been fun putting the question out there as I researched and wrote this book, for the reactions it generated. It has certainly made women stop and think.

The equality I feel in my own marriage—and the considerable effort my partner and I put into maintaining fairness and balance—is probably the main reason we've successfully survived as a couple for more than two decades. But I also firmly believe that the responsibility for placing value on my contribution to the partnership is *mine*. My partner has always believed in me, no matter what I was trying to accomplish. It's me that's always been the negative holdout.

"Simply put, marriage partners are only equal when *both* of them agree they are," Kathy, an American veteran of multiple moves, wrote to me. "It falls on the one who feels undervalued or stuck with all the mundane chores to make that position clear."

Although she describes her own marriage as old-fashioned and traditional, Kathy nonetheless feels like an equal partner with her husband despite their totally different work experience. "I've now found my niche doing research in my chosen field and following wherever that leads me. My husband supports this and manages very well to cook his own dinner when I'm out and turn a blind eye when the house becomes a mess."

One thing both Kathy and her husband do regularly is ask how they can help the other, she wrote to me. "So I sometimes end up picking him up at the train or mowing the grass, and he ends up doing a load of wash or picking up the groceries. We empathize with each other's circumstances and appreciate both contributions to our partnership."

"Marriage is an ongoing process," says the Institute for Equality in Marriage. "As your relationship grows and changes, make sure that one constant is equality." In a relocating world, where the only certainty is often *uncertainty,* ensuring your marriage strives for consistent equality is an important goal.

NOTHING MAKES A MARRIAGE feel unequal faster than the way household labor is divided. During the relocation process, as we've seen, an accompanying spouse will immediately notice the inequity when she gets stuck with a higher percentage of the couple's *home* work.

There are ways to rectify inequities in marriage, according to William J. Lederer and Don D. Jackson in their timeless marriage classic, *The Mirages of Marriage.*

One significant way, according to the authors, is for each spouse to stick to the roles for which he or she is best suited, regardless of customs or traditions dictated by society.

During our many relocations for the Canadian foreign service, it was always my husband who compiled the inventory of our belongings, originally as a painstaking handwritten document, later using a computer program designed for that purpose. No way was I taking on that task, not only because I don't like that kind of work but because my highly organized husband is definitely better suited to it. I have also been known to bolt out of the house with the kids, one step ahead of the movers, leaving him to mop up.

Similarly, since my partner likes to relax by cooking (he wooed me with food), it's completely logical that we reverse the traditional roles in the kitchen. What woman would be crazy enough to say to her husband, "Dear, please stop cooking all those delicious gourmet meals!" (And stop collecting fine wines while you're at it!) I've learned to shrug off the steady stream of jokes about the menus posted on our refrigerator notice board. (Would I make that up?) When family or friends have gushed over his lovely meals, then looked at me and said, not very diplomatically, "So, what do _you_ do?" I've refrained from pointing out the obvious: my husband is cooking because this happens to be the forty-eight-hour period he's in town. Don't get me started on what _I_ do to keep the home running.

Although it may be hard to avoid falling into those stereotypical 1950s gender roles created during a relocation, the authors of _The Mirages of Marriage_ believe that if a marriage is to be successful, "not only the assignment of roles, but other traditional attitudes and practices as well, must be revised." If you have a problem with your partner feeding or diapering the baby, or grocery shopping and cleaning, *get over it.*

You can't have it both ways, complaining that your husband doesn't do his fair share but then preventing him from trying to help out. Remember the couple in chapter 6 who had a child with special needs? The wife admitted she wasn't asking her husband for help, but when she did he was ready to jump in. Let your husband feel useful too, even if he decides to reorganize your kitchen cupboards without advance warning and you can't find anything afterwards. (It's amazing how many times I heard that story during my research.) Go out and smell the roses (or the coffee), then put the kitchen back the way you want it when he leaves on his next business trip.

THE QUID PRO QUO rule works to balance many marriages. Literally, *quid pro quo* means "something for something." In marriage terms, according to the authors of *The Mirages of Marriage*, it's an important process towards achieving a sense of equality. Leaving my husband to pack up with the movers while I went on ahead to the new place, for instance, was one way of balancing out my disappointment in always moving to Asia and never having the opportunity to experience other parts of the world.

"The *quid pro quo* process is an unconscious effort of both partners to assure themselves that they are equals, that they are peers . . . It is a technique which enables each partner to preserve his or her dignity and self-esteem.

Their equality may not be apparent to the world at large; it may be based upon values meaningless to anyone else, yet serve to maintain the relationship because the people involved perceive their behavioral balance as fair and mutually satisfying," write Lederer and Jackson. "Once the *quid pro quo* pattern has been established and accepted . . . each partner can live from day to day with some sense of security because he [or she] knows what to expect from the other partner."

In relocation, where women often end up spending six months or more selling the house, packing up, and looking after the children while the husband goes on ahead, the idea of a *quid pro quo* can head off resentment before the move has even taken place.

When Deirdre, a British accompanying spouse, wrote me to say that she was exhausted at the thought of doing just that—organizing an entire domestic relocation herself—I suggested she tell her husband that, once they were moved, she'd like to go off with her girlfriends for a holiday. The mere idea of it worked wonders for her frame of mind.

In chapter 5, I laid out the *quid pro quo* agreement I reached with my husband when I became so frustrated with trying to find meaningful work that I couldn't take the thought of any more rejection. The "something" I gave him was the "born-again spouse," whom I claimed would be happy to look after hearth and home. The "something" I got back was the freedom to write *and* peace of mind. No money changed hands in that transaction, but it wasn't long before we started *holding* each other's hands again.

Yvonne made a similar arrangement with her husband,

to the satisfaction of both. "In exchange for my availability to move all over the world for his career, I wanted the financial flexibility to establish a career working from home without the pressure to earn money. I had carefully thought out a new career for myself (as a researcher), and I wrote up a business plan covering everything I would need to get that career off the ground . . . The flexibility of my career meant he would never have to worry again about me forcing him to choose between his career or mine because I didn't want to relocate."

The *quid pro quo* Yvonne and her husband worked out in their marriage took some time to accomplish. "At first, we simply didn't have the skills or experience to know what we were addressing, how to address it, or even *why* it was important to think about these issues," she wrote. The solution came only once they'd stepped outside traditional ways of seeing their relationship. "It took me a while to figure out that all I had to do was alter my thinking. Once I changed my thinking, I set about helping hubby alter his. Getting him to see me outside of the traditional box I'd always been in was crucial to the success of my three-year strategy for myself. Altering his thinking didn't happen overnight, but when it did, it made a *huge* difference."

EVERY *QUID PRO QUO* comes with a few relationship rules, and trouble can occur when those rules are violated by either party. Significantly for our discussion, rules can also be easily broken by unexpected factors or pressures outside the marriage. Like a relocation, perhaps?

According to the authors of *The Mirages of Marriage*: "In the formulation of these rules, each individual must feel he [or she] has a right, equal to the other's rights, to determine what goes on. A person who feels he [or she] is being controlled, denied the rights of reasonable self-determination, will fight—overtly or covertly—to regain control." Been there, done that, for sure.

Like anything else in life, rules are irrelevant unless they are agreed to by both partners and then acted upon in the new context. Wrote Yvonne: "The rules won't change anything if we're still measuring ourselves against the way we used to measure success and happiness. I think when both spouses accept that success and happiness can be defined, and then redefined, quite differently for each other as the years and circumstances go by, that's when *quid pro quo* translates into a harmonious partnership based on growth and respect rather than a competition to see who's getting the fairer deal.

"Part of achieving that," she strongly believes, "is the woman's ability to let go of being the eternal victim (the 'why are you always doing this to me' routine) and to instead accept that forced changes often translate into a much more interesting and satisfying life. They certainly have for me."

Remember, too, that change involves adjustment, especially when a power imbalance is being redressed. After a dozen years in the American foreign service, and a lot of soul-searching, Helen decided that, when her husband's current assignment ends, she wants to settle down for a very long time back in the United States. Many of the things in life that are important to her (including her sanity) are simply not compatible with moving all the time.

"Basically, I hit a crossroads in my life, and chose not

to sacrifice any more of it to my husband's career," she wrote, echoing the words of other women I interviewed. "While my husband is truly agreeable to this in many ways, for reasons both personal and professional, I have noticed that lately *he* has started to play the victim! It's really annoying, and definitely goes to show that women are not the only ones who can be whiny about things when they don't feel like they have complete control over their lives."

NEGATIVE FEELINGS ALWAYS INTENSIFY when life seems out of your control. This happens as much in the day-to-day life of any marriage as it does during a relocation. But when, as often happens, both partners start feeling out of control during or after a move, marriage *repairs* can play a key role in swinging the relationship back over to the positive side, according to Dr. John Gottman, author of *The Seven Principles for Making Marriage Work*.

"A *repair attempt* refers to any statement or action—silly or otherwise—that prevents negativity from escalating out of control," writes Dr. Gottman. He believes that repair attempts are the secret weapon of emotionally intelligent couples who are first and foremost friends.

"These couples tend to know each other intimately—they are well-versed in each other's likes, dislikes, personality quirks, hopes, and dreams. They have an abiding regard for each other and express this fondness not just in the big ways but in little ways day in and day out."

Marriages typically start off with a high degree of positivity, according to Dr. Gottman, and neither partner can imagine their relationship turning sour. But, "over time anger, irritation and resentment can build to the point that the friendship becomes more and more of an abstraction . . . Eventually they end up in '*negative* sentiment override.' Everything gets interpreted more and more negatively." His comments describe some moveable marriages rather accurately.

I'm not sure my husband and I qualify as an emotionally intelligent couple, but when we were caught up in a tidal wave of negativity before our last move to Seoul, we came up with a "repair effort" that not only worked for us but was guaranteed to throw us into fits of laughter, always a healthy thing.

In the months leading up to our move, we didn't need "repairs" to our marriage but a full-blown restoration. We were communicating very badly, and no matter how we began our conversations, we ended up drowning in a sea of perceived criticism on both our parts. So what did we do?

We created imaginary placards that read: "This is not a criticism!" We pretended to hold up these signs before *any* conversation about the relocation. If we were discussing the flights we could take to get to Korea, I would hold up the imaginary sign before launching into *my* choice of airline or dates or route, to ensure my husband understood at the outset that I was not criticizing *his* choice of a travel itinerary for the family. If we were going to be talking about Korean language classes, my husband would hold up his pretend sign first, so I could learn about the availability of training without feeling any reproach about my complete inability to learn foreign languages.

We knew our repair attempt was working after dinner with good friends before our departure. They had laughed at our new way of communicating, yet the next thing we knew, when they proceeded down a dangerous conversational path in their own marriage, they too were holding up the imaginary signs!

You hear a lot about the importance of communication in happy marriages, but there's another message marriage professionals have for couples: you and your partner need to learn to communicate *properly*. Otherwise, communicating may actually make matters worse.

There's no one way to achieve effective communication. But I do want to highlight the need for it and outline a few kinds of communication that may do more harm than good.

Dr. Alan Solomon, a clinical psychologist with more than twenty years of experience working with families in southern California, believes expecting or demanding that each partner respond to a conflict in the same way is unrealistic. "Even after years of marriage, people do not think the same, have exactly the same values or priorities, or even respond emotionally in the same way to a set of circumstances," says Dr. Solomon.

"Communication is a process which takes effort, a lot of work at times, and almost constant refinement, adjustment and self-reflection. When things are going well, we take it for granted, relax, and ease up, which can then result in an explosive downturn when we don't expect it. Ongoing attention to this effort is very important."

One suggestion from Dr. Solomon is that it's better to communicate in an *assertive* way than an *aggressive* way, especially when talking about one's needs. As I've noted earlier, your husband is not a mind reader, and you are responsible for letting him know what you need. But it's very important to communicate your needs in a non-aggressive way.

What are those needs again? Here's my own top-five list:

1. *Consultation*

A woman who's consulted and brought into discussions about the move by her husband, his employer, or preferably both will feel she's being acknowledged as a key stakeholder in an event that will affect her life more profoundly than it does any other member of the family.

But never mind that it's a polite and civilized gesture: a woman *deserves* to be asked first. Numerous studies have demonstrated how much more successful a move is when the accompanying spouse is consulted.

2. *Respect and support*

The word "respect" covers a lot of ground, but a marriage without respect (on the part of both partners) won't survive a move. The unique concerns of the accompanying spouse *need* be respected. Long gone are the days when anyone—company, husband, relocation expert—could throw up their hands and say they didn't realize a wife would have her own concerns.

Everyone is well aware of the spouse's issues by now, and they've run out of excuses for ostrich attitudes. The needs of the spouse must be acted upon, whether the issue is a work permit or simply a polite response (instead of a blow-off) to an e-mail sent to the company for information.

At the same time, women *must* begin to express themselves and ask for this respect and support from their husbands instead of resorting to martyrdom or victimhood.

3. Equality

Equality in a moveable marriage is not measured by currency. A spouse needs to feel valued for her contribution to the move. This has nothing to do with money and everything to do with sharing power and operating like a team. Although society may use coin as the measuring stick, that won't work in a moveable marriage. A wife must feel valued, and this won't happen until both her husband and the spouse herself believe in her worth.

At the same time, a wife can't relegate her husband's needs to the bottom of the barrel. Equality means that you *both* count.

4. Certainty

A wife needs to feel certain she can trust her husband to stay faithful and loyal during a relocation and not run off with a new local colleague.

And as she becomes financially and emotionally more dependent on her husband, a spouse must know she has an escape route from the marriage if she desperately needs one. Often, a verbal contract isn't enough. A postnuptial agreement that stipulates a spouse will be compensated properly for giving up her own earning power can help ensure that if she is left high and dry after a move, she can find lawyers and retraining programs to put her shattered life back together.

5. Love

I've saved the best for last. We all need to be loved, unconditionally if possible. If a woman is going to throw away a stable life to support the career of her husband, she needs to know she is loved, and she should hear it and be shown it as often as possible.

Likewise, if a husband must make a move to support his career and his family, he needs to know *he* is loved, too. When love flows both ways, it's amazing how strong the relationship can grow.

WHAT MAKES A MARRIAGE a happy one? Recent studies have shown that the key to marital longevity is *endurance*. Couples who tough out the more difficult years of their marriage actually end up being happier than those who divorce over problems. According to researchers, the most common reason married people are happier is that they have stubbornly outlasted their problems.

I decided to write this book about moveable marriages to encourage that stubborn streak, to make couples aware of their unique challenges, and to point them towards ways of getting over the marriage hurdles often set higher by relocation.

My husband and I may have jumped off the relocation circuit when he left the foreign service for the private sector. But our marriage—along with my professional life and the way we raised our children—was, and continues to be, shaped by our mobility. Like the vows of marriage itself, I've learned that a moveable marriage is for keeps. The impact of any profound change never disappears. Traumatic change—and relocation is right up there on the list, along with divorce and death—is life-altering. It will forever define a person as well as a relationship.

Your moveable marriage will last a lifetime if you're lucky and if you work hard at it. Despite all the down days and the moving traumas, the constant change created by mobility is a good thing, in my opinion. For me it has meant growth and opportunity as an individual and, most definitely, as a spouse in partnership with the man I love.

resource guide

Books

Marriage

Gottman, Dr. John, and Nan Silver. (2000). *The Seven Principles for Making Marriage Work*. Three Rivers Press. ISBN: 0609805797.

Hanauer, Cathi. (Ed.) (2002). *The Bitch in the House: 26 Women Tell the Truth About Sex, Solitude, Work, Mother-hood, and Marriage.* William Morrow & Co. ISBN: 0066211662.

Krasnow, Iris. (2001). *Surrendering to Marriage: Husbands, Wives, and Other Imperfections.* Miramax. ISBN: 0786862181.

Lederer, William J., and Dr. Don D. Jackson. (1968). *The Mirages of Marriage.* W.W. Norton & Company. Reprint edition (January 1990). ISBN: 0393306321.

Pease, Barbara and Allan. (2001). *Why Men Don't Listen and Women Can't Read Maps: How We're Different and What to Do About It.* Broadway Books. ISBN: 0767907639.

Reeder, Roslyn M., and Chris Roerden. (1999). *Divorcing the Corporation: One Woman's Fight to Save Her Family from Multinational Maneuvers.* Hapi House Publishing. ISBN: 0966658604.

Roiphe, Anne. (2002). *Married: A Fine Predicament.* Basic Books. ISBN: 0465070663.

Romano, Dugan. (2001). *Intercultural Marriage: Promises and Pitfalls.* Nicholas Brealey Intercultural. ISBN: 1857882938.

Relationships, Change, and Inspiration

Bridges, William. (1980). *Transitions: Making Sense of Life's Changes.* Perseus Publishing. ISBN: 0201000822.

Engel, Beverly. (2001). *Loving Him without Losing You: How to Stop Disappearing and Start Being Yourself.* John Wiley & Sons. ISBN: 0471409790.

Lerner, Dr. Harriet. (1989). *The Dance of Intimacy: A Woman's Guide to Courageous Acts of Change in Key*

Relationships. HarperCollins. Reprint edition (April 1990). ISBN: 006091646X.

Steinem, Gloria. (1992). *Revolution from Within: A Book of Self-Esteem.* Little, Brown & Company. ISBN: 0316812404.

Career-Related

Crittenden, Ann. (2001). *The Price of Motherhood: Why the Most Important Job in the World Is Still the Least Valued.* Owl Books. Reprint edition (January 2002). ISBN: 0805066195.

Hertz, Rosanna. (1986). *More Equal Than Others: Women and Men in Dual Career Marriages.* University of California Press. Reprint edition (February 1988). ISBN: 0520063376.

McKenna, Elizabeth Perle. (1997).*When Work Doesn't Work Anymore: Women, Work, and Identity.* Delta Books. Reprint edition (September 1998). ISBN: 0385317980.

Parfitt, Joanna. (2002). *A Career in Your Suitcase 2.* Summertime Press. ISBN: 0952945347.

Relocation

Cummings, Dr. Barbara. (1999). *Sociological Impact of Corporate Relocation on the Family System.* Dissertation. com. ISBN: 1581120532.

Hickman, Katie. (1999). *Daughters of Britannia: The Lives and Times of Diplomatic Wives.* HarperCollins. ISBN: 0002557142.

Pascoe, Robin. (1993). *Culture Shock! Sucessful Living Abroad: A Parent's Guide.* Times Editions, Singapore. ISBN: 1957331966.

———. (2000). *Homeward Bound: A Spouse's Guide to Repatriation.* Expatriate Press. ISBN: 0968676006.

Marriage-Related Websites

American Women Overseas, *www.awoscentral.com*
A virtual online shelter for American women who are victims of domestic violence abroad.

DearPeggy.com, *www.DearPeggy.com*
A website that deals with and offers support to women whose husbands have engaged in adultery.

Expat Expert, *www.expatexpert.com*
This is my website, which has a links section filled with expatriate websites.

Institute for Equality in Marriage, *www.equality inmarriage.org*
A website devoted to helping women build equality in their marriages and recover from divorce.

International Divorce Law Office, *www.international-divorce.com*
The website of Jeremy Morley, a British lawyer based in New York City with experience in international divorce.

The Trailing Spouse, *www.thetrailingspouse.com*
The website of Yvonne McNulty, an academic researching spousal issues as they relate to mobility.

about the author

 Robin Pascoe is well known to traveling spouses internationally for her humorous, compassionate, and encouraging presentations to expatriate communities, human resource groups, and corporate gatherings around the world.

As well as writing countless articles and making many media appearances, Robin has written three previous books on the subject of global living and adjustment. Her personal experiences of packing and unpacking her life, marriage, and family throughout Asia were the inspiration for exploring the challenges and joys inherent to the expatriate lifestyle. Her popular website, *expatexpert.com*, is a treasure trove of information, opinion, and humor for expatriate couples. Robin currently lives in North Vancouver, Canada.

praise for robin pascoe's
previous books and website

"I just wanted to write a short note to say thank you for your wonderful website. Now that I've discovered *expat-expert.com* I really feel I've been thrown a lifeline!"
~ ANGELA SAVORY, ONTARIO, CANADA

"When I began reading *Homeward Bound*, I was amazed to see that almost every feeling, fear, and frustration that I have experienced was described as if it was my own personal journal. I laughed, I cried, and I read passages out loud to my husband, who was desperately trying to get some sleep. I can't tell you how much it helped to hear your 'voice' echo my feelings so well."
~ MELINDA ENNIS-ROUGHTON, ATLANTA, GEORGIA

"I felt Families in Global Transition was an excellent conference in so many ways. Those who did not attend it really missed out. My favorite was Robin Pascoe. She is my kind of woman. I got all three of her books and am deep into reading them. I now have a new hero!"
~ LOIS BUSHONG, COUNSELOR

"You have made a difference in so many people's lives. I give your books to anyone I know who is facing a move—just knowing your feelings are normal and shared is wonderful. At least if corporations are still lousy, you are filling the need. Keep it up!"
~ CHRIS HEWITT